A Better Woman

Simon Mendes da Costa

GREENHEART PRESS

First published in 2023 by

Greenheart Press (Greenheart Press Plays)

Copyright © Simon Mendes da Costa 2023

Simon Mendes da Costa has asserted his moral right to be identified as author of this Work in accordance with sections 77 and 78 of the Copyright, Designs and Patents Act 1988

A CIP catalogue record for this book is available from
the British Library

ISBN 978-0-9571829-7-4

Produced by The Choir Press

Cover Design by Paul Baker of A Stones Throw

Caution

All rights whatsoever in this play are strictly reserved. Application for professional or amateur performing rights etc. should be made before rehearsals begin to the author c/o Greenheart Press, 25 Douglas Avenue, Whitstable CT5 1RT, Kent, UK.

No performance may be given unless a licence has been obtained

This book is sold subject to the condition that it shall not, by way of trade or otherwise, be lent, resold, hired out, or otherwise circulated in any form of binding or cover other than that in which it is published and without a similar condition being imposed on the subsequent purchaser

Simon Mendes da Costa trained at the Bristol Old Vic Theatre School and worked as an actor for a number of years before turning his hand to writing. His first play, *Table for One,* was performed at the Hen and Chickens Theatre in 2001 *(Time Out's* Critics' Choice). His second play, *Losing Louis,* earned him a nomination for the *Evening Standard's* Most Promising Playwright award. It premièred at Hampstead Theatre in 2005 directed by Robin Lefevre and starred Lynda Bellingham and Alison Steadman. The production transferred to the West End before embarking on a No. 1 UK tour. A separate, Americanised, production opened on Broadway at The Biltmore Theatre in 2006. *A Better Woman* was commissioned and premièred at The Marlowe Theatre, Canterbury during Simon's tenure as Literary Associate.

Other publications by Simon Mendes da Costa

Losing Louis published by Methuen Drama (2005)

ISBN: 9780413775122

For Emma

the inspiration for this play before we even met

The world première of *A Better Woman* was presented by The Marlowe Theatre, Canterbury, on 1 December 2015. The cast was as follows (in order of appearance):

Morris	Paul Panting
Sherry	Charlie Norfolk
Tom	Ben Porter
Jessica	Alexia Traverse-Healy
Julia/Dates	Poppy Miller
Directed by	Tilly Vosburgh
Designed by	Liz Ascroft

This playscript contains significant changes from the original production.

Characters
All characters are between 35 and 45
Morris
Sherry
Tom
Jessica
Julia (Paula, Nadine, Catherine and Amelia are all played by the actor who plays Julia)

Setting

An Edwardian semi-detached house in Chiswick, West London.

The stage is initially set as a kitchen/living room in the process of being decorated.

Large dust sheets cover what we imagine to be furniture and these dust sheets can be removed at times to reveal other locations.

The play takes place over one week in early January.

All transitions between scenes should be continuous and seamless.

Act One

Scene One

Tom's *house, early Saturday evening.*

Morris *enters in painting overalls. He's setting up to apply the first coat of paint to* **Tom**'s *house.*

Sherry *enters, getting ready to help.*

The door bursts open and **Tom** *runs in.*

Tom	I can't find my wallet! ... I can't find my wallet!
Morris	*(checks the time)* Christ. Better hurry.
Tom	She's in the car!
Sherry	Here?
Morris	Now?
Tom	Have you seen it?
Morris	What's it look like?
Tom	It's a wallet! *(frantically searches the room)* I definitely had it. I had it. Not there. No. Think. No. Not there. No. Where? Where?
Sherry	Bedroom?
Tom	Bedroom.

Tom *disappears upstairs.*

Morris *and* **Sherry** *run to the window.*

Sherry	What's she like?
Morris	Too much reflection off the windscreen.
Sherry	Let's see.
Morris	Christ, she's getting out.

They both duck down then sneak a further look.

Sherry Let me see.

Morris/Sherry *(both impressed)* Ooo. Woh.

Sherry Bit obvious though.

Morris Dreadfully obvious. She's magazine material.

Sherry Heels and jeans. Clever.

Morris I could sell that look.

Sherry She's way out of his league.

Morris That's worrying.

Sherry That is worrying.

Morris She's coming in. Sherry, she's coming in.

Sherry I can see that. Come on.

Morris No, let's –

Sherry Come on.

Morris Can't we just –?

Sherry No we can't just – *(calling upstairs)* Tom, she's coming in.

Tom *(offstage)* What?

Sherry She's coming in.

Tom *(offstage)* Who is?

Morris Who is? She is!

Sherry *(calling to* **Tom***)* We'll go round the back. *(to* **Morris***)* Come on. Come on.

Sherry *herds* **Morris** *out the back door.*

A few moments later **Jessica***, heels & jeans, dark glasses, mysterious and enticing, enters openly carrying* **Tom***'s wallet.*

Act One, Scene One 5

Crashing noises from upstairs.

Jessica *looks up at the ceiling, considers for a second, then pops the wallet in her bag and begins to inspect the house.*

Tom *runs in.*

Tom	Oh.
Jessica	Your doorbell doesn't work.
Tom	But aren't we –?
Jessica	I get lonely waiting in cars. Decorating?
Tom	Yes. New year, new start. You know.
Jessica	Did you know there are two workmen running across your lawn?
Tom	Oh yeah, they're the ones –, the ones who are, er, helping. My neighbours.
Jessica	Didn't have to leave on my account. *(looking at the painted tester squares on the wall).* That's the one. Why do you have a Stannah stair lift?
Tom	My mother –
Jessica	*(alarmed)* You live with your mother?
Tom	No. She died.
Jessica	Sorry. When?
Tom	About five years ago.
Jessica	Why haven't you got rid of it?
Tom	Well, we're all getting older.
Jessica	Right. *(seeing a framed photograph of **Tom**'s ex on the wall)* And who do we have here? Nice picture.
Tom	My neighbour, he's a photographer.
Jessica	Jack of all trades. But who's the pretty subject?

Tom	Um well, she's –, erm, Julia … um, she was my –
Jessica	New year, new start. Why do you think most people do internet dating?
Tom	To meet a partner I would guess.
Jessica	God, I doubt it. Must be loads more reasons than that. Boredom. The thrill of the chase. Desperation.
Tom	I'm not desperate.
Jessica	Loneliness. Revenge.
Tom	Revenge?
Jessica	Sex.
Tom	Well, ultimately obviously but not straight away.
Jessica	My guess is you're a third date sort of guy, maybe fourth, whereas I'm a first date sort of girl. First or never. I either know or I don't.
Tom	Isn't it funny we're having this conversation and we haven't even gone on our first date yet?
Jessica	I think we're on it, though. Don't you? Don't you think it's only after sex that you get to know someone, before that your mind's too clouded with if you're going to or not. Nice house this. Do you want children?
Tom	What!?
Jessica	How many dates have you been on?
Tom	I don't know.
Jessica	Come on, how many?
Tom	Not sure, about twenty I suppose.
Jessica	Twenty? This is only my second.
Tom	Oh. What was the other one like?

Act One, Scene One 7

Jessica Dull.

Tom Oh dear.

Jessica Oh don't worry, you're not dull. You're funny.

Tom I am? Not sure I've been described as that before. And in such a short period of time.

Jessica Doesn't take me long.

Jessica *(has found the fridge underneath one of the dust sheets)* You really do like a fridge magnet. 'Cats have nine lives which makes them perfect for experimentation' Ha!

Tom I'm sorry I really can't find it.

Jessica Don't worry I'll pay.

Tom I couldn't let you do that.

Jessica Don't be so old fashioned, you can get the next one.

Tom *(addresses the audience for the first time)* What did she mean by that? I'm not good with reading signs. That seemed like she'd –. But how could she? I've only just picked her up from Chiswick station. Not that that's relevant.

Jessica *(still reading the fridge magnets)* 'Always remember to remove the bell from a cat's collar before you cook them' ... 'Every time you masturbate God kills a kitten'.

Tom God, sorry, I'd forgotten about that one.

Jessica Must be a right blood bath in here sometimes. I don't much like cats either.

Tom Oh.

Jessica The classic dog or cat question, I'm a dog.

Tom God, you're not.

Jessica Spontaneous and emphatic. Bodes well.

Tom But I do have a cat. Tilly. She'll be around somewhere. I inherited her but she is pretty much mine now.

Jessica *(one she already knows)* 'If you don't talk to your cats about catnip who will?' How long you been doing this dating stuff?

Tom Couple of months.

Jessica And twenty dates? You must be exhausted.

Tom I am a bit, yes. I had hoped to have tied it all up before Christmas.

Jessica What, didn't fancy pulling your own cracker?

Tom Maybe.

Jessica Sigh of relief from the kittens. And you haven't found anyone you like? There must have been one or two that were OK.

Tom There were plenty that were OK. But OK isn't OK.

Jessica Ah, a perfection seeker.

Tom There's nothing wrong with striving for the best. But I have been told that I've been approaching it in the wrong way. So now I am being –, new year, new start, I'm being less fussy.

Jessica I'm flattered.

Tom No, no, no, less, er, specific in my requirements.

Jessica Right. So how do you know when the perfect person comes along?

Tom I'll just know.

Jessica So when she walks in that door, how long will it take you to know?

Tom I wouldn't know straight away, how could I? Well, I might know no, but I won't know yes.

Act One, Scene One

Jessica Interesting. ... So what do you normally do on these dates? Drink? Meal?

Tom Yes.

Jessica Do you always pay? I bet you do.

Tom Not always, depends if I want to see them again.

Jessica Do you tell them that beforehand? How exciting when the bill turns up.

Tom No. I pay if I don't want to see them again. Makes me feel better about not picking them.

Jessica Not picking them. That's hilarious. How many have you wanted to see again?

Tom Two. But they didn't want to see me.

Jessica Perhaps it's because you made them pay.

Tom No, we split it. I didn't want to set a precedent.

Jessica A precedent? You should go on the telly.

Tom They seemed more than happy to pay half.

Jessica You just get funnier and funnier. Do you know anything about women?

Tom Very little, so it would seem, but I believe in equal rights.

Jessica Excellent. Well done.

Tom *(he means this)* Too often women allow themselves to be subjugated by the men they're with. They let themselves be dictated and ruled rather than take their rightful place alongside. They should have equal opportunities, equal pay and afforded the same respect for bringing up children as a property mogul is for producing millions.

Jessica Gosh.

Tom   Don't get me started on equal rights.

Jessica   I won't.

Tom   And if you really want to know. I *am* in it to find a partner. Someone to share my life with. Someone I can love and someone who'll love me back. I'm sorry if that's an old fashioned idea but I believe in it and I'm not going to give up until I find it.

One truth deserves another.

Jessica   I have a child.

Tom   Oh.

Jessica   Yes.

Tom   It –

Jessica   No, it didn't say. It puts most people off. Ella's her name, she's twelve, and on a sixpence can slide seamlessly between Postman Pat and Priti Patel. Her father, I'm divorced, hasn't been with us since she was a baby. I should have said. But something about you appealed and I wanted the chance.

Tom   Wow.

Jessica   And cards completely on the table. I'm 36 not 34, *(referring to her youthful looks)* yeah I know. And my dream would be to have a little brother or sister for Ella before it gets too late.

Tom   Heavens.

Jessica   Does that put you off?

Tom   Um.

Jessica   I'll go. It was wrong of me not to have told you. I was being underhand. I thought it best I came clean before things progressed.

Tom   Progressed? Oh. Yes.

Jessica	I can understand you wanting to leave it now. There aren't many men who can take on a situation like this. I understand if that's not something you're able to do. Should I go?
Tom	Well, we both should. We have a date to go on.
Jessica	Thank you. Yes we do. *(a genuine moment of tenderness ... leading to :-)* Fancy doing some charlie instead?
Tom	What?
Jessica	Coke. Cocaine.
Tom	Drugs?
Jessica	Oh come on don't look so shocked. Have you got a mirror? ... Oh, your wallet. It fell out in the car. Hey, what's to lose.

Jessica *hands* **Tom** *his wallet.* **Jessica** *exits into the hall.*

Scene Two

Tom's *house, the next morning (Sunday).*

Morris *enters ready to help decorating.*

Morris	Cocaine?
Tom	Cocaine.
Morris	Did you?
Tom	I was shocked.
Morris	But did you?
Tom	It just came out of nowhere.
Morris	So did you?
Tom	But the real problem is that she's got a twelve year old.
Morris	Did you like it?
Tom	Which she lied about on her profile.

Morris You've said. But what about the drugs and the sex?

Tom She doesn't want me to meet her yet.

Morris Tom?

Tom She says it's too upsetting to meet men who then disappear.

Morris That makes sense. But what was it like?

Tom I mean that's a thoughtful thing I think.

Morris Very. What was it like?

Tom It was fantastic.

Morris Was it. Bet it was.

Tom Too fantastic. I won't be doing it again. Very disturbing. She doesn't do it very often, she just had some left over from a christening she went to before Christmas.

Morris A christening?

Tom She thought it was a good way of breaking the ice. Which it did.

Morris I bet it did.

Sherry *enters.*

Tom But she's got a child.

Sherry Who has?

Morris The bird he was shagging last night.

Tom I didn't say I was shagging her.

Morris You didn't say you weren't.

Sherry It's not all about getting your end away, Morris.

Morris Of course it is.

Sherry Boy or girl?

Act One, Scene Two 13

Tom   Girl. Ella.

Sherry   Nice name.

Tom   It's a lovely name, I thought that, she's twelve.

Sherry   Well, that's a good age, get in before they go completely off the rails.

Tom   And she's very immediate.

Sherry   Who is, Ella?

Tom   No, Jessica.

Sherry   Jessica's the –?

Morris   Yeah, the one he was –

Tom   I didn't say I was.

Morris   You didn't say you weren't.

Sherry   What happened to Veronica?

Morris   Forget Veronica we're on Jessica now.

Sherry   I liked the sound of Veronica.

Morris   Veronica's history, Sherry.

Tom   Veronica! Yes. You know all about compatibility.

Morris   She deals in divorce.

Sherry   I deal in preventing divorce.

Tom   Veronica was nice though. Maybe I should ask her out again.

Morris   Hang fire, you've been rabbiting on about this Jessica girl for half an hour straight. And once you've slept with them you're duty bound to give them a second chance.

Tom   I didn't say I'd slept with her.

Morris	You didn't say you didn't. And that car never moved once it came back. Is that what you mean by immediate?
Tom	No. It's that she just comes right out and says things she's thinking.
Morris	How dreadful.
Tom	She doesn't have a censor button. Things just blurt out.
Sherry	Like Julie Andrews. ... In the Sound of Music ... That's why she was thrown out the nunnery.
Morris	Unless Julie Andrews wanted to do drugs.
Sherry	No!?
Morris	Straight up. One minute she was telling him she had a child.
Tom	Which she lied about on her profile.
Morris	Next minute she was racking a line out.
Sherry	*(looking at **Morris**)* Racking a line out?
Morris	That's what you call it, apparently.
Sherry	What did you do?
Morris	He did it.
Sherry	No.
Tom	Alright. I'm not that square.
Sherry	Oh you are Tom.
Morris	Sherry, this woman's good for him. Perhaps you and me should do drugs.
Sherry	*(correcting his grammar)* You and I. Yes. She sounds fun.
Tom	But you just said about Veronica.

Morris	Maybe she has Tourette's.
Sherry	Maybe she's just what you need.
Tom	What, a drug taking, nymphomaniac?
Morris	Ha! I knew it.
Tom	I mean the bottom line is. What I'm now thinking. Is that I'm quite happy being on my own.

Sherry and **Morris** *instantly burst out laughing at this.*

	OK I'm not but what about the twelve year old girl? Who she lied about?
Morris	Wonder why she did that?
Tom	I wasn't looking to have other people's children in the equation. I don't know anyone who is.
Morris	There's a clue.
Tom	I know at this stage it's unlikely I'm not going to have to deal with all that.
Morris	True.
Sherry	Yes.
Tom	I mean if she's worth having other people may have –
Morris	– had her.
Sherry	She's lit a fire in you.
Tom	But is it the right type of fire?
Morris	Bit out your league if you ask us.
Sherry	He's gorgeous, what are you talking about, nothing a few new clothes won't fix.
Tom	I don't dress well, do I?
Sherry	Not really. No.
Morris	Just get in there and see where it goes.

Morris *exits.*

Tom   What, just see where it goes?

Tom *looks at* **Sherry** *for help.*

Sherry   You already have the wisdom. You just need the courage to find it.

Sherry *exits.*

Tom   *(to the audience)* I kissed Sherry once. It's not what you're thinking, we were nine. It was in the playground, during school lunch, and we were playing 'True love, dare, kiss or promise'. It must have sparked something in her, it certainly sparked something in me, because later that afternoon I received a note, delivered by her best friend Elizabeth Crisp, who had a lisp, funny, that I was to meet her in the woods on the way home. They weren't really woods as such more a clump of trees separating the road from the park. But it's where you went. There was the odd dodgy bloke hanging around who'd probably be in prison today but apart from that it was relatively private. So at just gone three thirty, I was shifting from foot to foot, waiting, as directed, by the burnt out tree. I thought it might all be a joke, which would have been a relief and I was just about to leave when out of nowhere she appeared. Not sure how long she'd been there. She hesitated then edged across to me and stared at the ground. I had no idea what I was supposed to do, and horrifyingly it appeared that she didn't either. We half glanced at each other for a bit, quite a bit, until eventually she said that we could play a game. Which was a relief. Until it turned out to be the 'If you show me yours I'll show you mine' game. Apparently I had to go first. Which I did. Then she screamed and ran off. She didn't have any brothers. It turned out our meeting was merely to satisfy her

Act One, Scene Two 17

emerging curiosity. And she never kept her side of the bargain.

Sherry *enters, carrying her overalls and a tin of paint.*

Tom Sherry?

Sherry Yes.

Tom *looks at her for a moment too long* What?

Tom I was thinking about –, cancelling my other dates.

Morris *enters ready to start painting.*

Morris There's more?

Tom I'm trying to get this sorted. Once and for all. And move on. Then I can start living. Properly. Like you. Plan stuff. Go on holiday. Have dinner parties. What if my second date with Jessica didn't match up to my first? And I've cancelled these others. I'd have to go back and start all over. So not unreasonable to go. Would it?

Morris What do you reckon, Sherry?

Sherry *(referring to the paint they've chosen)* I think it maybe too brown.

Morris No! We've decided.

Tom Yes, I've been thinking that too.

Morris Now look what you've done. It's a lovely colour.

Sherry Bit more brown than I thought.

Morris It's golden. It says it's golden. Golden Symphony. It always looks different in the tin. It'll dry lighter.

Sherry Brown.

Tom And Sherry's right, I've been looking at it again. If you come over here and see it towards the door. Can you see what I mean?

Morris No. No I can't see what you mean.

Tom The colour of the hall changes it. I'm not sure I like that colour as much. I like it from over there towards the window.

Morris Well, stand over there then.

Tom I can't always stand over there, can I?

Morris But how often are you going to stand over here with your cheek pressed up against the wall. ... We looked at all those tiny cards for weeks and we arrived at our top five. And there they are. The ones you stared at, you glanced at, caught them by surprise, held up cushions to. You even put on your favourite shirt to see if it clashed and eventually we picked this one. Let's at least bloody paint it and see.

Pause.

Tom *(pointing at another painted square)* Jessica thought this one.

Morris That's the one you ruled out first.

Tom She said it would work well with the blinds.

Sherry She's got a point.

Morris But no vote. Not yet, obviously. Look there's barely much between any of them, it doesn't matter, we've picked this one.

Tom But I could change it.

Morris No. No, you can't change it.

Tom I'm going back to bed.

Morris *(referring to the decorating)* But what about –?

Tom Just a couple of hours. ... What's wrong with the colour it was?

Tom *exits.*

Act One, Scene Two   19

Morris   I don't know. What's wrong with the colour it was?

Sherry   Racking a line out? ... You haven't? Have you?

Morris   Ah. Something about me you don't know?

Sherry   Is there?

Morris   Could be. ... Maybe.

Sherry   Nah. ... Nah.

Tom *enters unable to let it go.*

Tom   Look. Listen. She was –, in your face, didn't shut up, challenging everything I said. Took the piss out of me. Mercilessly. OK, so maybe she was attractive, had a certain something, a sparkle, an energy, something I've never experienced before. Which was, yes, exciting, I suppose. Yes and alluring and compelling. Yes. But she wasn't my type. That's what I'm saying. There may be better people out there. For me.

Sherry   There will always be better people out there. For anyone.

Morris   What?

Sherry   No, not us.

Morris   What are you saying?

Sherry   What are the chances out of eight billion people she's your perfect match?

Morris   For anyone?

Sherry   No. No. I don't mean that. Because there's no such thing. Is there?

Morris   Isn't there?

Sherry   Perfect comes from being there, going through stuff. You make it perfect. You can't start perfect.

Morris   Right.

Sherry   And at some point you've got to stop looking or you'll go mad.

Tom   But what if one of the ones I cancel *is* my perfect match? Think about that. I'll have discarded my destiny.

Sherry   What are the chances, Tom?

Tom   They're none if I don't go.

Sherry   And what about all the others that you haven't even looked at yet? They could be your perfect match.

Tom   Christ. They could.

Sherry   This Jessica though –

Tom   But you thought Veronica.

Sherry   Veronica's history, Tom! Jessica sounds fun. She may just be good enough.

Tom/Morris   Good enough?

Morris   Not very romantic.

Tom   I can't bring up someone else's child. It's not part of my plan. I must honour the dates I've booked. And if they're no good, I'll then give Jessica a proper go.

Sherry   Be sure to tell her that.

Tom   So I need a quick way to rule each one out.

Morris   Ask to see a picture of her mother. *(in answer to* **Sherry***'s look)* Your mother's hot.

Sherry   If you like the look of her then just find out if she's kind.

Tom   Simple as that?

Sherry   Kindness is underrated.

Tom   Right. Thanks.

Act One, Scene Two

Tom *exits to bed.*

Morris He's never going to land such a peach without a few drawbacks.

Sherry You think she's a peach?

Morris *lifts up a corner of a dust sheet and takes out* **Tom**'s *iPad.*

Morris You said yourself she was out of his league. Without a child in tow she'd command a higher prize than Tom. He'd just be 'good enough'.

Sherry That's not what I meant.

Morris Lookie here.

Sherry Is that Tom's?

Morris *(referring to the iPad)* He really does need to get some security.

Sherry Are those his —? You can't look at those. We mustn't look. No —

Morris — we mustn't. These are the ones. Look, Paula.

They start scrolling through **Tom**'s *forthcoming dates.*

Sherry We really shouldn't be —. Ooo. Paula. Hello Paula. She looks —

Morris What?

Sherry Up front.

Morris Accommodating, perhaps. Wednesday Nadine. Looks posh.

Sherry Very posh. That's not Primark.

Morris What's the most important characteristic in a woman?

Sherry For a man? That's —

Morris No, what a woman thinks a man should want.

Sherry What's the point in that? They don't want what we think they should want.

Morris But what do you think we should want?

Sherry It's irrelevant. What does a man think a woman should want in a man?

Morris That's easy. Not too tall, slightly going to seed, thinning hair but very funny and very sexy.

Sherry Thinning?

Morris Thinning. And good enough.

Sherry *(in agreement)* Good enough. ... Ah Amelia. She looks nice.

Morris Mmm. Yes. She looks lovely.

Sherry She does indeed.

Morris Amelia, yes. What does that say when the sexes agree? Too perfect perhaps.

Sherry Hang on a sec.

Sherry *flicks back and forward on the screen.*

Morris What?

Sherry Don't you think they all look – ? Maybe –. A bit, on the similar side.

Morris Yeah. I suppose they do in a way. Yeah, they do a bit.

Sherry Apart from Jessica.

Morris Oh yes, definitely the odd one out. Oo look, another Paula.

Sherry Another –

Sherry *and* **Morris** *continue looking at the iPad ...*

Scene Three

Bistro, Monday evening.

Tom *and* **Paula** *are revealed sitting in a restaurant.* **Tom** *is half asleep.*

Tom   *(coming to : as if remembering her name)* – Paula.

Paula   What?

Tom   Paula.

Paula   Were you asleep?

Tom   No. Just resting my eyes. Bit of a heavy weekend. More coffee? *(referring to the wine)* Or would you like to finish the –? Oh it's finished. Would you –?

Paula   I think I've had enough. Don't want to behave inappropriately. ... Though we could have a small one for the road.

Tom   We should get them to book you that taxi.

Paula   In a minute. Oh, may I have my photo back? I like a man who's interested in family. Kindness *is* an underrated quality. ... You never finished telling me your hospital story.

Tom   Yes, well, I survived. Touch and go for a bit. Everyone says '*chew it*' to me now, '*chew it*'.

Paula   Chew it. You make me laugh.

Tom   Do I?

Paula   Yes. Haven't done much of that recently. Laugh.

Tom   Oh. Really? You seem quite a happy person.

Paula   Well, I suppose I am tonight. I suppose sometimes you're not because you're –, well –, you know. ... Save that for another time. ... Assuming there is another time. ... Life isn't always –. Well, it is I suppose, but not always, can't always be. Can it? But tonight it is, yes.

Tom   Well, that's good. *(looking at the bill)* And this is –. Yes. Let's have a look at this, then. Yes. It was a very nice evening.

Paula   It was. It is. Lucky you didn't go for the steak.

Tom   *(still looking at the bill ... deciding)* Yes. Chew it. ... Look there's something I've been meaning to tell you all evening and I feel I ought to come clean.

Paula   Oh. Here we go. I knew this was too good to be true. Nice guy. Intelligent. Single. Sorry to tell you dear but I'm gay.

Tom   Gay?

Paula   Let me tell you you're not the first.

Tom   Who's gay?

Paula   My husband.

Pause.

Tom   You have a husband?

Paula   Ex husband. Soon to be ex husband.

Tom   You're still married?

Paula   There wasn't a box to tick for soon to be single. So what's your secret?

Tom   And he was gay?

Paula   It's not so uncommon these days. It's what happens, you get married, promise to be together forever, have children, then your husband gets spotted tossing off blokes in toilets. It's mundane.

Pause.

Tom   You have children?

Paula   Come off it. That was on there.

Tom   Was it?

Tom *gets out his phone.*

Paula   I'd hardly lie about having kids.

Tom   *(getting her details up on the Dating App)* It doesn't say here.

Paula   Where? *(he shows her)* That's not me.

The scene fades and **Tom** *addresses the audience.*

Tom   *(to the audience as he looks at his phone)* That's not her. How did that happen? So who's this? *(he flips through the Dating App and finds her)* Oh yes, flash twice.

Scene Four

Tom's *house, late Tuesday evening.*

Morris *and* **Sherry** *drinking wine.*

Morris   How was Paula number two?

Sherry   Up front?

Morris   Accommodating?

Tom   What happens to women when they get older?

Sherry   They become more intelligent, wise, sensual, more profound, with a heightened cognisance and forgiveness of male imperfections. Why?

Tom   We met in a car park off the A13. She had an old red Nissan Cherry with a dented wing, we'd previously exchanged number plates. Not that we needed to, the place was deserted. I'd been there about ten minutes hoping I'd been stood up because I'd decided I was definitely going to tell this one straight away about Jessica, and move on with her, Jessica, once I've finished all the other dates, when suddenly I hear Tina Turner blasting out at full volume, a good ten seconds before her car squeals in through the barrier. She flashes twice and hand brake turns to a halt in front of me.

Morris   In a Nissan Cherry?

Tom   I was about to get out to explain when she just took off again, honking her horn and gesticulating for me to follow. I could barely keep up, we were doing more than sixty round all these country lanes. Then as we round this corner my heart sinks as I see her turning into the car park of the biggest Wetherspoons pub I'd ever seen.

Sherry   Oh dear.

Tom   Which also happened to be her local.

Morris   She brought you to her local?

Tom   We park and I'm expecting this blowsy rock chick when instead a rather overly prepared East End secretary type gets out. Dark jacket, white, slightly frilly blouse. Cleavage.

Morris   Uh-huh.

Tom   And short skirt. Very short. She spent most of the evening tugging it down.

Sherry   So you told her immediately about Jessica.

Tom   Well ... I do later bring up the Jessica situation, which she listens to and asks me why I'm here then.

Morris   So what did you say?

Tom   What could I say? I told her the truth.

Morris   That you were seeing if there was anyone better out there.

Tom   No. I said it was already booked and it seemed rude to cancel at such short notice. She accepts all this with a smile.

Sherry   And then you leave.

Tom	No, there was this two for one meal deal and it seemed rude not to. We had another drink. The pressure's off and we're having a lovely time.

Morris	Right.

Tom	Suddenly she's really funny, and more interested in everything I'm saying. Thought my choking incident was hilarious –

Morris/Sherry Chew it.

Tom	– refused to let me finish my meal, took my plate away, and even gave me the Heimlich Manoeuvre as we left. Which is when I became aware that she might have wanted to kiss me.

Morris	How did you become aware of that?

Sherry	Come off it Morrie, how does anyone know about these things.

Tom	In fact I think she might even have wanted me to go back home with her.

Sherry	Well, how did you know that?

Tom	She said so.

Morris	And you went.

Tom	No.

Morris	Why not?

Tom	Because of Jessica.

Morris	You turned down a shag?

Sherry	He wants a relationship.

Morris	No! You can have the relationship afterwards.

Tom *moves away.*

Tom	*(to the audience)* I was frightened tonight. I was frightened of going back with her. I pretended it was a moral decision but it was fear. I think she just fancied having sex, simple as that. Women who behave like men are scary. I was scared. Scared of the –, can't even say it. I'm pretty good at sex, I think, once I get going, once I relax, once I know someone but –. ... I always think women must think it's a reflection on them. I'd have been a much happier woman. Julia was amazing, our first time together, she made me feel like an emperor. She told me a year later it was all an act but she got us over the hurdle. I haven't been with someone new in years. Can't get any easier. Can it?

Tom *exits.*

Morris   He's probably getting more sex than we are.

Sherry   Still think it's a bit brown.

Morris   Needs a second coat.

Sherry   Which'll make it more brown. ... We did the right thing, didn't we?

Morris   What about?

Sherry   We didn't give up too soon. Trying.

Morris   How dare you say that.

Sherry   Sorry.

Morris   After all you –, after all we –

Sherry   Yes.

Morris   My balls ache even at the memory of that procedure.

Sherry   Sorry, yes. And it wouldn't be reversible now anyway. Would it?

Morris   Stop it.

Sherry   Sorry. *(referring to the profile pictures)* Does that similarity of look remind you of anyone?

Morris   Should it?

Sherry	Look at Nadine here. *(about what she's just said)* Sorry.
Morris	What am I looking at?
Sherry	Her nose and the mouth. This bit.
Morris	Difficult to see with the chin strap.
Sherry	Where's the other one?
Morris	That's a mighty big horse. Here she is skiing. Fancy going somewhere different this year, on holiday?
Sherry	Oh. Really? But we like –
Morris	Yeah we do but we could maybe –
Sherry	This one.
Morris	Sipping Pimms at Henley.
Sherry	That look.
Morris	What, that smug entitled look?
Sherry	The picture of his you took.
Morris	What about it? What am I looking –? Oh God. Julia?
Sherry	Julia.

Lights dim on **Morris** *and* **Sherry**.

Scene Five

Tom's *house, Wednesday evening.*

Tom *and* **Nadine** *are sitting waiting to be seated, menus open.* **Nadine** *has a flute of champagne and* **Tom** *a lager in a tall elegant glass.* **Nadine** *is studying her menu.*

Tom *(to* **Nadine***)* I'm completely over her anyway. You have to be, don't you? I mean you love their memory of course. So –

(to the audience) It was meant to be a surprise for Julia. It was. I opened the bedroom door and there they were.

> I saw her. She saw me. He was otherwise engaged. I jumped back and shut the door. I couldn't move. Just standing there holding this gigantic Easter egg. And then I became aware of something. They hadn't stopped. They were still at it. After a bit I tapped on the door. I thought maybe she *hadn't* seen me. She told me later she had. She just said it was difficult to bring him to a halt. So –
>
> *(continuing to* **Nadine***)* – I wouldn't be doing this unless I'd put it behind me. You can't move forward otherwise, can you?

Nadine *looks up from her menu, having not taken in anything* **Tom** *has been saying and continues with her previous conversation.*

Nadine Angus, my ex, well, ex ex, there was an ex in between, he wasn't much better. ... In the generosity department.

Tom She actually saved my life once. I was choking on a piece of –

Nadine I think it may be a gene in men that's either there or it isn't, I could never date a tight man again.

Tom This is a lovely place you've brought us to.

Nadine Keep it under your hat but they're in line for their second Michelin star.

Tom Second? Bit greedy.

Tom *opens his menu, knows it's going to be expensive but is still visibly and audibly shaken.*

Nadine What? Seen the lobster? Yes, it's their signature dish.

Tom Though the soup also looks good.

Nadine Ha. ... So Tom let's cut to the chase.

Tom About what?

Nadine What you're looking for and am I it?

Act One, Scene Five   31

Tom   We haven't even got to our table.

Nadine   It's well known you make up your mind about someone within the first fifteen seconds.

Tom   Do you?

Nadine   In the old days we'd have looked across a crowded room, caught each other's eye and known straight away. So am I in or am I out?

Tom   God, that's a bit –, I could ask you the same question.

Nadine   Go on then.

Tom   Am I in or am I out?

Nadine   You're out.

Tom   Oh.

Nadine   Don't take it the wrong way you're just not my type.

Tom   Aren't I? What is your type?

Nadine   Taller probably. Younger. More rugged. Square jaw type.

Tom   Right.

Nadine   Call me shallow but that's what I like.

Tom   You did look at my profile?

Nadine   Yes but thought I'd give you a chance to disprove my prejudice, sadly you didn't.

Tom   Oh. OK. Right.

Tom gets up and prepares to leave.

Nadine   Where are you going?

Tom   Well, I just thought that –

Nadine   That's it?

Tom   What's it?

Nadine	No fight. No, 'I'm great, wait till you get to know the real me'. 'I'm dynamic, sexy, fantastic in bed'. Nothing?
Tom	What?
Nadine	I'm messing with you. Play the game. Sit down.
Tom	But –. Well, I am great, and er you don't know the real me and I'm –
Nadine	You can't just repeat it back. Sit down.

Lights come up on **Sherry** *and* **Morris**, *both scenes are now in play.* **Tom** *is in both.*

Sherry	You didn't sit down?
Tom	Then she says.
Nadine	Kiss me.
Morris	Oh my God.
Sherry	After all that?
Tom	She was beginning to scare me.
Sherry	Beginning!?
Nadine	Kiss me, you can tell a lot by a kiss.
Sherry	Tell me you left.
Morris	Tell me you didn't.
Tom	*(to the audience)* I was torn.
Nadine	There's no-one looking.
Sherry	She's plainly mad.
Morris	But gorgeous and rich.
Nadine	Kiss me.
Sherry	You didn't?
Morris	He did.

Act One, Scene Five   33

Tom *(to the audience)* All last night I was thinking I should have kissed Paula and I didn't. I should have swept her up and taken her home and shagged her. And shagged her.

Sherry Please say you didn't.

Tom *(to the audience / **Morris** & **Sherry**)* It started off alright. But as she warmed up it kind of increased. Until it was like kissing an overripe guava.

Morris Guava?

Tom Slobber and tongue. So much tongue.

Morris Guava?

Tom No subtlety.

(to the audience) But to be honest really rather erotic.

*(back to **Morris** & **Sherry**)* Then it was over and she gave me a quizzical look. I couldn't work out whether she was pleased or disappointed. I couldn't move. Then she stands up and –

Nadine *gets up walks off, just before she exits, she and **Tom** together mime the hand/ear 'call me' sign.*

Tom *(very angry with himself)* I was within a hairsbreadth of leaving and she turns the tables and rejects me. I didn't want to kiss her.

*The restaurant is now gone and **Tom** is fully with **Morris** and **Sherry**.*

Morris Didn't you?

Tom I feel like I've been disloyal to Jessica. Should I come clean?

Sherry/Morris No!

Sherry Christ no. Stop kissing mad women though.

Tom Yes. I'm very sorry. I didn't mean to. I'm exhausted.

Tom *makes to exit.*

Morris *(regarding the decorating)* But –

Tom Sorry.

Tom *exits to bed.*

Morris Is he *ever* going to pick up a paintbrush? ... So he's trying to replace Julia, is he?

Sherry Subconsciously.

Morris Well, apart from her doing the dirty, you can hardly blame him.

Sherry Oh I know *you* liked her. Took enough pictures of her.

Morris You liked her too. She was lovely, a little complicated perhaps.

Sherry Nicely put.

Morris I was showing her how to construct a good photograph.

Sherry With her as the subject.

Morris I do people. I was simply helping her get in to photography.

Sherry Get into skimpy outfits more like.

Morris Does a gynaecologist get turned on by looking at a fanny?

Sherry Don't say fanny.

Morris What would you prefer me to say, –

Sherry *(cutting him off before he is extremely crude)* No! I wouldn't prefer you to say anything. I just don't like the word fanny.

Morris You're a funny one. What's wrong with fanny?

Sherry Stop it.

Act One, Scene Five   35

Morris I'm a professional photographer.

Sherry So was David Bailey.

Morris I'm not David Bailey.

Sherry No.

Morris Anyway she's gone and Tom is on his own, he does have get out there. Risk all this. Otherwise what would be the point to his life?

Sherry What do you mean?

Morris He's got a dead end job. Making boxes.

Sherry Designing boxes.

Morris Imagine that on the careers evening at school. Wouldn't be many at that table. So with no wife or kids it's like, if he'd never existed, it wouldn't have made much difference.

Sherry We don't have kids.

Morris No, I know but –

Sherry Is that what you think about us?

Morris No, of course not, we're married aren't we? You have a job that helps people stay married and I have a –

Sherry You said kids.

Morris I didn't mean just –

Sherry But you said it. No wife or kids.

Morris Or kids. ... I didn't mean just kids.

Sherry Is that all it's about?

Morris Not just. It's not like we didn't try.

Sherry So what have we done?

Morris You and me are a team.

Sherry *(correcting his grammar)* You and I. Yes.

Morris Together we make a difference. I just meant Tom needs to do something, be someone or he'll fizzle like the Neanderthals and the Duck Billed Platypus.

Sherry You mean the Dodo.

Morris Michelangelo had no kids and he left us David and the Sistine chapel.

Sherry And we're painting a suburban semi brown.

Morris Golden. ... How often do you think we do it? *(no reply)* Sex.

Sherry I knew what you meant.

Morris I heard once that if you put a pebble in a jar every time you did it during your first year together and then took one out for all the times you did it after that –

Sherry – you'd never empty the jar.

Morris So I started to jot it down. ... When we did it.

Sherry You've been keeping a log?

Morris Wouldn't call it a log as such.

Sherry *(refuses to be drawn)* So aren't you interested?

Sherry No.

Morris Oh. OK. *(pause)* Once every nine days if you must know. On average. More in the summer.

Sherry There you are then.

Morris Aren't you horrified?

Sherry How often do you want to do it?

Morris At least twice a week.

Act One, Scene Five   37

Sherry   Twice?

Morris   It actually works out about 40 times a year, we'd have knocked that off in a month once.

Sherry   Bollocks.

Morris   Without sex a relationship can become more fractious.

Sherry   What? But ours isn't without sex.

Morris   Yeah but I thought considering what I'd –

Sherry   *(jumping on this)* Considering what you'd what?

Morris   Nothing.

Sherry   I bet if you asked most people of our age if they did it more than once a week –

Morris   Nine days.

Sherry   – they'd laugh at you.

Morris   Sex isn't an optional add on it's the glue that keeps it together.

Sherry   What the fuck have you been reading?

Morris   Everything off your shelf.

Sherry   Jesus, Morrie.

Morris   Well, fuck you too.

Sherry *picks up the iPad and attempts to get* **Morris** *to look at another profile picture; he's having none of it.*

Sherry   What, don't want to play anymore? Catherine. Yes. Older. Been round the block I think. A more mature version of Julia. Yes. That's something at least. Divorced. What d'you think? Oh come on. Shut up, I'll give you a – *(she politely mimes giving him a hand job)* if you're that desperate.

Morris   I'm not desperate. I don't want a stupid –

Sherry	So what do you think?
Morris	Fanny. Fanny. Fanny.
Sherry	Baldy.
Morris	Oh hilarious. ... Cosy.
Sherry	Cosy? Is that really your best shot? I'm not cosy.
Morris	Cosy.
Sherry	I'm not cosy. (**Morris** *exits wiggling his bum and imitating* **Sherry** *being cosy*) Oh very mature.

Lights dim on **Sherry**.

Scene Six

Restaurant/Bar with a dance floor, Thursday evening.

Tom *hasn't been following the conversation as well as he might.*

Catherine Well, yes, that's precisely what we are. Just because things don't happen when they should. Not everyone wants them anyway. I didn't. Could be considered a bonus. Right? As the hot flushes hit you have to accept where you are in life. And men get stuff too, whatever age. Have you achieved enough, what's your legacy, are you still potent.

Tom Potent. Yes.

Catherine And no-one talks about it.

Tom No?

Catherine I can't even discuss it with my girl friends, they're all in denial, cause they're so young, such a young crowd. Age is so arbitrary, don't you think. You know even my doctor is embarrassed by the symptoms.

Tom Is he?

Act One, Scene Six

Catherine Well, he's a man, can't shoot him for that, much as we'd like to, but I blame women, we've just got to stand up and shout about it. Do you find tampon adverts embarrassing?

Tom Sorry?

Catherine No, but I bet you did. When they first started. Now they're commonplace we don't care, that's what's got to happen.

Tom *still looks confused.*

Catherine With the menopause.

Tom *(as if he knew all along)* Exactly.

Catherine We have to make it just part of life. I'm through the worst now. I mean it happened exceptionally early for me, obviously, which was a shame, a great shame, but it doesn't make you less attractive, does it?

Tom No. ... No.

Catherine And men get physical symptoms too, you know, the male menopause, it's not a myth.

Tom Isn't it?

Catherine Loss of sex drive. Ability. Been there worn that T shirt. And you can get hot flushes –

Tom Can we?

Catherine – and mood swings, not just women. Loss of muscle mass, fat suddenly appearing where it wasn't before, tiredness, dry thin skin, increased sweating –

Tom Yeah.

Catherine – poor concentration, irritability, loss of enthusiasm. Prostate problems. Incontinence. Need I go on?

Tom Well, maybe ...

Catherine Craggy old decrepit men are considered distinguished and wise. Why? Your wrinkles and lines indicate wisdom, ours decay? It's just a matter of perception. I mean how people see you and how they see me is different.

Tom I'm not wise.

Catherine No, or you wouldn't have had the steak.

Tom Chew it.

Catherine But you are distinguished.

Tom And you're lovely.

Catherine Lovely? Oh dear, kiss of death. Oh well. It's just not fair. Women are defined by their child bearing ability and that was OK once, when we all died at fifty.

Tom Right.

Catherine So it shouldn't matter, should it?

Tom What?

Music starts up.

Catherine Oh my favourite. Come on let's dance.

Catherine *(gets up and dances her way off)* HRT is a fucking life saver.

Tom *moves across to* **Sherry**.

Scene Seven

Tom's *house, late Thursday evening.*

Sherry *is clearing up.*

Sherry Is it?

Tom That's what she said. I never knew the Menopause was such a big deal.

Sherry No.

Act One, Scene Seven 41

Tom The last great taboo. No-one speaks about it. Women don't even talk to each other. Is that true?

Sherry Why are you asking me?

Tom We've all got to shout about it, take away the stigma. Not be embarrassed by the symptoms.

Sherry Did she –?

Tom You don't know the meaning of the word flattened until you hit the menopause.

Sherry Right.

Tom One minute you're walking along all fine, next it's like you don't exist, you're invisible, you can't remember anything, you can't concentrate.

Sherry Oh.

Tom She got depressed and scared.

Sherry About what?

Tom No idea. Then she started getting bitter and angry and didn't know why.

Sherry Shit.

Tom But she has got her sex drive back.

Sherry Did she lose it?

Tom Must have done.

Morris *enters.*

Sherry How old was she?

Tom Forty five.

Sherry Fuck.

The phone rings.

Tom I'm not here.

Tom *exits.*

Morris *(incredulous to **Tom**'s lack of helping)* Where's he going?

Sherry You're right, Morrie.

Morris About what?

Sherry Us not having enough sex.

Morris What's brought you to that conclusion?

Sherry I'm not immune to a well constructed argument. *(she answers the phone)* Hello. Tom Edward's residence. ... It's Sherry. ... I'm his next door neighbour. We're helping him decorate, not that *he's* doing much. ... God no, though he did kiss me once in the playground. ... Yes, embarrassing, right bang in the middle of the playground. ... Ha. No that is definitely not a euphemism. Are you Jessica by any chance?

Morris Don't ask that. It might –

Sherry Thought so. ... He's out I'm afraid. ... Hang on a second.

*(to **Morris**)* Have we seen a red high heeled shoe?

*(to **Jessica** on the phone)* We're just having a look.

*(**Tom** arrives back)* Oh Tom's just come in.

*(to **Tom**)* Hi Tom! ... It's Jessica.

Tom *(taking the phone)* Hi Jessica, hi, how are you? ... Did you? ... Oh yes I remember.

*(to **Sherry**)* It's in the fridge.

Sherry The fridge?

Sherry *fetches the shoe.*

Tom   The ice making compartment.

(*to* **Jessica**) I'll bring it with me. ... Ha. ... Yes. Unless you get cold feet. Ha. Sorry. Yes, that was a bit lame. Ha. Bye. Bye.

Morris Did she actually laugh at that joke?

Tom   Yes.

Morris Marry her.

Tom   Yes! You're right. That's it. Marry, that's the answer. That's what women want, the commitment. It's all about that. I've one more date and then I'm going to commit.

Morris To Jessica?

Tom   I'm going to commit. I am.

Sherry Calm down. Don't think about commitment just yet.

Morris Take it easy mate. One step at a time.

Tom   No. I must.

Morris You've only shagged her once, it's not –

Tom   I haven't shagged her once!

Morris Alright. Easy.

Tom   How many times!? We never had sex. I told you. Once you do everything changes. You're sort of committed then, aren't you?

Sherry Committed to what?

Tom   Well, to, er, them.

Sherry Oh. Right. Are they committed to you?

Tom   Yes. No. Yes. Well, it's a bit different for women.

Sherry Is it? I'd have thought the opposite.

Tom Yes, the opposite I suppose, that's what I mean, different, so they still retain the option.

Sherry I don't follow. To do what?

Tom To decide.

Sherry They're not committed?

Tom No. Because they've –, because they've –, given. Haven't they?

Sherry They've given? And you've –?

Tom Yeah.

Sherry Taken? ... They're grown women.

Tom God. I just want to be with someone I already know. Is that too much to ask? Evenings in watching the tele. Boring stuff. That's what I want. I want to have what you two have. I want to be bored. It's so difficult. How did you two manage to make that leap?

Sherry I got pregnant.

Sherry *exits.* **Morris** *goes after her.*

Tom *(to the audience)* I'd forgotten that. ... I often wonder what would have happened if our kiss in the playground had been the beginning of something bigger. My life would have been much simpler. I could be cosying up on the sofa with Sherry listening to Morris's problems. ... I would have forgiven Julia if she'd wanted me to. We're all entitled the odd slip up. That sort of thing destroys some blokes, not me. Don't get me wrong I didn't want it to happen, and in my own bed. But I wasn't consumed by the 'it' as such until I realised the 'it' meant something. I'm more like a woman that way. I may have said. ... It was all my fault anyway. I introduced her to Geoff, my boss, at the Christmas party, they got on immediately, like they'd met in a previous life or something. She said she'd spent the whole night talking about me and bigging me up. It certainly worked because I was suddenly promoted to supervisor, which meant I had to work longer hours. Which meant he often had to, kindly, pick Julia up from the station for me and take her home. My fault not marrying her at the beginning when she wanted it. When all was new and the romance was fresh. Miss the moment and it's gone forever. So I'd get home and they'd be on their second bottle, of my Meursault. And he'd end up sleeping on the sofa with me going to bed before them.

Tom *exits.*

Scene Eight

Tom's *house, Friday evening.*

Sherry *enters,* **Jessica** *follows her on.*

Jessica I thought as I was passing.

Sherry No problem. It's here somewhere.

Sherry *looking for the shoe, lifts a dust sheet and pulls out some stuff,* **Tom**'s *iPad comes out amongst it.*

Jessica I expect Tom's told you all about our little date the other night.

Sherry No. Not really.

Jessica Liar. So he's out.

Sherry Yes. Not sure where.

Jessica Tell him I dropped by. Though I don't want to seem like a stalker.

Sherry He should be so lucky.

Jessica He should. He's a nice guy. Well, you should know, he kissed you in the middle of the playground.

Sherry	Ha. No, not a euphemism. It was a while ago though. ... Hah.
Jessica	What?
Sherry	Just remembering that day. ... Oh I know where I put it.

Sherry *exits to fetch the shoe.* **Jessica** *waits, she sees the iPad, gives it a touch without expecting anything and is suddenly confronted with the profiles of the other women, transfixed, she looks at them and remains on stage as the next scene unfolds.*

Scene Nine

Restaurant, Friday evening.

Tom *and* **Amelia** *at the end of their meal.* **Tom** *has just finished telling his choking story.*

Tom	So you'd've –?
Amelia	Well, I am a doctor.
Tom	So you are, I'd forgotten. *(they both laugh)* Amelia is a very pretty name.
Amelia	Thank you.
Tom	And here's the bill.
Amelia	Before you say anything, we're splitting this. No argument.
Tom	Actually I was thinking the same.
Amelia	*(playing at being affronted)* Oh, were you now?
Tom	Don't want to set a precedent.
Amelia	Indeed.
Tom	I was also thinking it would be lovely to see you again.
Amelia	I thought you might be thinking that.
Tom	How did you think that?

Act One, Scene Nine 47

Amelia Just a hunch. And I'm delighted. But now comes the hard part.

Tom Why?

Amelia You're actually the first person I've had to say this to. Which is a compliment.

Tom Is it?

Amelia I've decided that I don't want to spend the rest of my life alone.

Tom Well, who does?

Amelia Hence the reason for embarking on this tortuous succession of dates.

Tom I couldn't agree more. Not that this one –.

Amelia No. But it's exhausting getting to know new people. I want to be with someone I already know.

Tom Oh my God. I was just saying exactly that.

Amelia Were you?

Tom I was.

Amelia But to get what I want I've had to, and I apologise for this, engage in a little subterfuge.

Tom You're 40 not 35.

Amelia No, I'm 35.

Tom You have an undeclared child.

Amelia No.

Tom Your husband's gay.

Amelia What?

Tom Some of the things I've encountered.

Amelia Heavens. Really? No. I don't have a husband.

Tom Good.

Amelia And if I did, he wouldn't be gay.

Tom How could he?

Amelia But –, because if I hadn't and you'd known the truth I don't believe we'd be sitting here now. So I'm sorry for my deceit.

Tom I'm intrigued.

Amelia I don't think there are many people on this planet, whoever they are, that would choose to be on their own.

Tom You're very pretty, as well as your name.

Amelia Thank you. Unfortunately. Unfortunately I can't say how long I've got to live.

Tom Pardon.

Amelia Just sucked the life out of the room, haven't I?

Tom No. No.

Amelia I have MS. Not quite sure how aggressive. Could be twenty years before I'm laid low. Perhaps more. Could be five though. Perhaps less. Actually you know what. I'll get this. *(she takes the bill)* Think about it.

Amelia *exits.*

Tom *(to the audience)* I thought she was going to say, she used to be a man. I wasn't expecting that. Well, it would have been a strange thing to be expecting, wouldn't it? I wanted to see her again. I feel now like I should see her again. I did want to. I mean none of us know when we're going to die. We could walk away from here and just keel over. Tonight. We think we won't but one day we'll be wrong. Let's face it we are all going to die.

Tom *exits.*

Scene Ten

Tom's *house, Friday evening.*

Sherry Found it.

Sherry *returns with the shoe and gives it to* **Jessica**.

Heels and jeans. It's a good look. If I ever leave Morris that's what I'll be wearing. Sorry but when you've been married as long as we have vicarious pleasure is all that's left.

Jessica Don't say that. You're what we're aspiring to.

Sherry I think since all this began with Tom, I think *you're* what Morris is aspiring to. Well, not you in particular. Oh, sorry, I shouldn't have said –.

Jessica Don't worry, I know this dating stuff means he's been seeing other people. Well, up to this point hopefully.

Sherry *(very slight hesitation)* Yes.

Jessica Not up to this point hopefully? There was a hesitation there.

Sherry No.

Jessica There was.

Tom *enters.*

Tom Oh Jessica, hi.

Sherry I'll er –

Sherry *exits back into the house.*

Jessica Just needed this. Didn't want to spend tonight limping. These are the only ones that go with my outfit.

Tom Tonight? You're going out tonight? Quite late.

Jessica Always been a night owl, me.

Tom I'm really looking forward to our date tomorrow.

Jessica	Me too. How have you been?
Tom	Good. It's been a crazy time at work.
Jessica	Making boxes.
Tom	Designing them.
Jessica	Designing them.
Tom	I'd have happily dropped it round to you if I'd have known you needed them so soon.
Jessica	No that's fine. Hope you didn't mind me –
Tom	No, not at all.
Jessica	*(referring to the fridge magnets)* How's the cat? ... Still alive?
Tom	What?
Jessica	Or is it just kittens?
Tom	Oh.
Jessica	Well, I look forward to seeing you tomorrow, north west corner of Tottenham court road and Goodge street, on the Pret a Manger side of Hamburger Union, under the sign everything starts with delicious meat. I shall be wearing a pink scarf for identification purposes ... oh, and this shoe.

Jessica *turns to go.*

Tom	I should have texted. Sorry.
Jessica	Should you? No, that's fine.
Tom	It was such a fun night the other night.
Jessica	Oh did you think so? Good. It was fun, wasn't it? OK. See you –
Tom	Would you like a drink?
Jessica	I need to get going.

Tom	Yes. Of course. ... Going anywhere nice?
Jessica	I don't know.
Tom	Oh. You don't know where you're going?
Jessica	Not yet.
Tom	It's always nice to be surprised. ... It's just so odd this stuff. I'm not used to it. People seeing people and then people seeing other people.
Jessica	Are you seeing other people?
Tom	No I meant, you seeing other people.
Jessica	Oh me. I thought you meant you. That you were seeing other people.
Tom	No. No that's not what I meant.
Jessica	Not what you meant or not what you're doing?
Tom	Not what I meant. Look, I'm sorry. I should have rung or texted or something. Probably not good form. I apologise. It's just if I'm honest I've been in a bit of a dilemma.
Jessica	About?
Tom	About um –
Jessica	Me?
Tom	No. No. Sort of. Not entirely.
Jessica	Go on.
Tom	This doesn't negate anything between you and me. It's just –
Jessica	– there's someone else.
Tom	To be honest I don't know. Look you and I had a great time.
Jessica	I thought so, yes.

Tom	But there'd been these other ones I'd sort of organised. And I thought –. And there was this one.
Jessica	Fine. Look it's fine. We've both got our eyes open. Tell you what. This one. Whoever she is. You're attracted to her?
Tom	I'm attracted to you.
Jessica	Good. Tell you what. How about this? Have you slept with her?
Tom	No, God no, that wouldn't be fair. I wouldn't be having this conversation if I'd slept with her.
Jessica	I think you should.
Tom	What?
Jessica	Date her, sleep with her, see if she's the right person and if she is, great and if not, give me a call. I'll be here. Not forever but for a bit.
Tom	Really? Sleep with her?
Jessica	I imagine you've slept with other women.

Jessica *makes to leave.*

Tom	Look I don't want to sleep with her. I want to sleep with –, go out with you.
Jessica	Tom, take your time.
Tom	No I definitely want to go out with you.
Jessica	Really. It's fine.
Tom	I want to go out with you!
Jessica	Well, if you're sure.
Tom	I am, yes.
Jessica	Well, that's lovely. I'll see you tomorrow.
Tom	Yes. Good. OK bye. And um –?

Act One, Scene Ten 53

Jessica Yes?

Tom Your thing tonight. Will you be um ?

Jessica What?

Tom Going?

Jessica Of course.

Tom Oh.

Jessica It's so rare for my dad to take me out these days.

Jessica *exits.*

Tom *(to the audience)* And there it was. The moment. The decision. Was that a decision? Or was that entrapment? I think she might be cleverer than I am. But what about Amelia? What if she'd put me on the spot? What do I want? What I think I want I don't get. But I don't know if what I think I want is what I really want. But I do want. Morris says if it wasn't for women men would still be living in caves. He says he's glad he doesn't live in a cave. I think I live in a cave.

Tom *exits.*

Morris *and* **Sherry** *enter, they have been waiting to leave.*

Morris Let's go, I'm starving.

Sherry I wasn't serious the other day. About the baby thing.

Morris Good.

Sherry I'm sorry. I haven't suddenly changed my mind.

Morris Well, that's lucky.

Sherry Morrie?

Morris Yes, I know you're sorry. It's fine.

Sherry Morrie?

Morris   Forget it, let's just go and eat.

Sherry   Morrie?

Morris   Please don't –

Sherry   Morris?

Morris   I'm hungry.

Sherry   Do you fancy taking a pebble out the jar instead?

Morris *takes a moment to realise what she's saying.*

Both exit next door in pursuit of satisfaction.

Scene Eleven

Tom's *house, Saturday evening.*

Jessica *&* **Tom** *run in from the rain.*

Jessica   Wow. ... I'm surprised you asked me back.

Tom   Why?

Jessica   You picked up the tab.

Tom   Second dates have different rules.

Jessica   Third date. I picked up my shoe remember.

Tom   Does that count?

Jessica   If you want it to.

Tom   Would you like some wine?

Jessica   I would.

Tom   Red or white?

Jessica   White please. I don't have any more coke by the way.

Tom   Chardonnay, Viognier, Sauvignon Blanc, Albarino or Riesling?

Jessica   Chardonnay.

Act One, Scene Eleven 55

Tom Unusual these days. New World or Burgundy?

Jessica Burgundy.

Tom Macon or Chablis?

Jessica Chablis. How many wines have you got back there?

Tom Just an Argentinian Malbec and a Spanish white. I'm trying to tell you I'm more fine wine than hard drugs.

Jessica I know. Come and sit down.

He doesn't sit.

Tom Tell me about your family.

Jessica Why?

Tom I don't know anything about you.

Jessica My dad's dead, my mum's mad. Come and sit down.

Tom Why is she mad?

Jessica You'll have to ask her that. Come and sit here.

Tom Your dad's dead?

Jessica Yes.

Tom You said you were going out for a meal with him.

Jessica I lied.

Tom So who were you going out for a meal with?

Jessica I wasn't.

Tom You made up a lie about going out for a meal and the person you invented to go out with was your dead father?

Jessica I was on the spot.

Tom But why the shoes?

Jessica I wanted to see you again before tonight.

Tom Why?

Jessica	To make sure.
Tom	Of me?
Jessica	Yes. Come and sit down.
Tom	When did your dad die?
Jessica	When I was seventeen. Sit down.
Tom	Did you get on well with him?
Jessica	I adored him. I worshipped the ground he walked on. Sit down.
Tom	Do you have a good relationship with your mother?
Jessica	What?
Tom	Even though she's mad?
Jessica	Have you seen Mommie Dearest?
Tom	Just Julia had an issue with her mother, don't think she ever had enough love and I sort of spent our relationship trying to make up for that lack. And failing.
Jessica	Interesting wooing technique, bringing up your ex's relationship with her mother.
Tom	People's relationships with their parents often reflect down into relationships with their partners.
Jessica	Do they? Right that's it, time to get serious.

Jessica *removes her blouse and then goes to remove her bra but never does.*

Tom	You haven't really told me about Ella.
Jessica	*(incredulous – referring this to her lack of attire)* You want to discuss my daughter?
Tom	It's just –.
Jessica	She's twelve and hates me. Sit down.
Tom	What happens if I sit down?

Act One, Scene Eleven 57

Jessica Tom. You could suck the fun out of anything. ... Actually so can I.

Tom I was just trying to slow things down for a bit.

Jessica Oh. You want to slow things down. Should I go?

Tom No. God no. Don't go. Anticipation that's all. I was playing with the joy of anticipation. You can never get this moment back, can you?

Jessica Why would you want to? It's horrible.

Tom Oh God do you think so too?

Jessica My feeling is it's like a plaster that needs to be ripped off.

Tom I always pull mine off slowly.

Jessica Stop trying to turn me on. Kiss me. Put your glass down and kiss me.

They kiss, it becomes urgent. She begins to unbutton his trousers.

Tom Arggh.

*(Action freezes. **Tom** extricates himself and comes forward to address the audience, one of his fly buttons is undone)*

This is the moment in the film when you neatly cut to post coital bliss. *I* want to cut to post coital bliss. Let's skip that bit in the middle. We're all waiting for it to finish so we can get on with the story. Aren't we? I am. It's too intimate, private, to be dissected in any way but with a general sweep. And then it's always wonderful or very very occasionally disastrous. And if it's disastrous, it'll be funny disastrous. There's not much mileage for OK ish. The sort of sex most people have when they first get together. This is supposed to the fun part. If only Julia hadn't left I wouldn't be going though all this. It's amazing the amount of thoughts you can have in the time it takes for someone to undo one button of your flies.

(undoes one more of his fly buttons) I should be getting back. I wonder what's going through her mind right now. I could ask her but it seems the time for chat has passed. Put up or shut up. I'm a man. This is what I want.

(has got himself back in position. The action restarts) Arggh. Look before we go any further can we have a talk about a few things?

Jessica   OK.

Tom   It's about what you said on our first date.

Jessica   Yes?

Tom   About maybe wanting to have another child.

Jessica   Maybe.

Tom   I thought we should talk about it.

Jessica   So soon?

Tom   No I mean –

Jessica   This is our third date, isn't it?

Tom   Yes.

Jessica   We haven't skipped forward six months and I've been in a coma.

Tom   No.

Jessica   And we've established you're a third date sort of guy.

Tom   Apparently so.

Jessica   Does the term getting lucky not appeal?

Tom   Oh God yes. Yes it does.

Jessica So why are we talking about having children?

Tom It's only cause you said –

She cuts him off with a kiss. He breaks it again.

Tom Should we have the sexual health discussion?

Jessica Oh God, should we?

Tom Well, what did you think was going to happen when we went upstairs?

Jessica Upstairs?! I was going to have you on the floor.

Tom Were you?

Jessica You've probably changed the sheets, though.

Tom Bit rude not to. Should we talk about safe sex?

Jessica Talk about it?

Tom I'm not very good with all that. Puts me off.

Jessica Puts us all off. Come here. Sit here with me. Have a sip of wine. ... Cheers. Now. Let's start again. How about we just sleep together and see what happens? Tell you what, how about we say the big prize is off the table tonight? We'll just take turns to award each other the runners up medal.

Tom Really?

Jessica Really.

Tom The runners up –?

Jessica Don't ask.

Tom No.

Jessica Happy?

Tom That is a relief.

Jessica For me too.

Tom Is it really? Good. I'm getting quite excited again.

Jessica Funny that. Come on. There's one thing I want to say though.

She picks up her wine and moves to go upstairs.

Tom What?

Jessica The lights stay off.

Tom Oh.

Jessica You can't see my stretch marks until date eight.

Tom Date eight?

They have exited.

After a short while a woman walks in carrying a small suitcase.

Tom *runs back on to fetch his wine.*

Julia Sorry. *(indicating the key in her hand)* The doorbell's broken. Is this a bad time?

Tom Julia!?

Blackout.

Act Two

Scene One

Tom's *house, a short while later.*

Julia *has been speaking for some time.*

Julia	..., it was beautiful. It had been a miserable day, pouring with rain, thunder and lightening all through and then, just then, the clouds parted and a shaft of light like a golden arrow broke through and lit up the brass handles as they were lowering her into the ground. Oh Tom, I know I should have called you.
Tom	No. But –
Julia	I know how much you loved her but I couldn't face it not with Geoff there. I couldn't deal with the two of you in the same place. I hope you understand.
Tom	Of course. But I need to say –
Julia	He gets so jealous. He got so jealous.
Tom	When?
Julia	When we were together.
Tom	You're not together?
Julia	We'd been on the slippery slope for ages and now with Mum dying it tipped us over the edge. You'd have thought it would have brought us closer. To be fair I have been hideous. I've been hideous with everyone. You know how hideous I could get.
Tom	No.
Julia	When we were together I was horrible. I'm sorry I was so horrible.
Tom	No.

Julia	If I could turn the clock back and not be horrible. I would. Why are we all so horrible to each other? Seeing Mum at the end I realised life can be beautiful and we spend it worrying about the most trivial things. I'm sorry I was horrible.
Tom	No.
Julia	Tom. Please. I'm sorry. Accept my apology. Please. I'm sorry.
Tom	Of course I accept it. Look –
Julia	I mean I know it wasn't all my fault.
Tom	No.
Julia	It never is, is it? Just one person. Always takes two.

Julia *inadvertently picks up* **Jessica***'s blouse and holds it throughout the rest of the scene.*

Tom	Of course. Thing is –
Julia	I was thinking about us as I watched the sun set over Buttermere and I thought –
Tom	Buttermere? In the Lake district?
Julia	It's where I've been living.
Tom	Is it?
Julia	And as the sun disappeared over the horizon I had this overwhelming sense that I needed to be here. Like I'd regret it if I didn't come.
Tom	Right. But the –
Julia	So I jumped in the car and here I am.
Tom	You've just driven here from there?
Julia	Did I do the wrong thing? Did I?
Tom	Well, –. I don't –. I don't –

Act Two, Scene One 63

Julia Because I can just get in the car and drive back and realise it was one of my mental aberrations. Julia going bonkers again. You used to call me bonkers, remember.

Tom Did I?

Julia Bonkers. I could be bonkers. You did love me though, didn't you?

Tom Yes. But you see –

Julia I know you did. And I jumped all over that love. I abused it. Though of course I wasn't entirely to blame.

Tom No.

Julia Both of us have to take our share of that.

Tom Of course we do.

Julia I mean you could be a bit distant at times.

Tom I'm sure.

Julia And getting the love word out of you was like getting blood from a stone. Even though I'm sure you did. Love me.

Tom Yes.

Julia Probably still do, I imagine, but events have happened. You can't expect things to go back to how they were in a moment of minutes, however much you might want them to.

Tom No.

Julia I started to wonder who left who.

Tom Did you?

Julia I know I went off with Geoff. That's probably how you remember it.

Tom   Yes.

Julia   But was the person who left really the one being left? ... I didn't want to sleep with Geoff.

Tom   Didn't you?

Julia   And how did I get to running a guest house? In the Lake District. So cold and miserable. It never stops raining. And I'm not an outdoor type. You know that. And you have to be, Tom, up there, you really have to be. Everyone is. Look Kendal Mint Cake.

(she produces some Kendal Mint Cake that gets put on the side)

And cagoules and fleeces are what passes for fashion. And all this was going through my mind as I drove down. What time breakfast was and how they want their stupid eggs. And was there really a pencil museum in Keswick? How hilarious. Do you have any more of those adorable little soaps? One wash and they're gone. God, you have to be so hospitable. All this was buzzing in my head. And you were, Tom. You were. All through the journey. And as I came off the motorway I cranked Coldplay up to full volume. 'Yellow', your favourite. And I thought about us seeing Paris and going to New York and it was going over and over in my mind. And that weekend in the Cotswolds. Over and over. Headlights were dazzling me, I could hardly see through the windscreen. Then suddenly there were flashing lights and before I knew it I was being breathalysed by a policeman young enough to be the son we never had. 'Calm down Madam' he kept saying, 'calm down'. Madam? When did I become a madam? 'Take a deep breath, all in one go'. I wasn't taking it in, kept sucking when I should be blowing. I'd been up over a hundred apparently and what with Coldplay and all the other stuff, they'd been behind me for miles. Luckily most of it had worn off and I just scraped under the limit. Then I was sobbing and a very nice police lady took my hand in hers. Beautiful hands. Gold band. Could I lie down for a while, I haven't slept?

Tom   Um.

Julia   I've got nowhere else to go.

Tom   Well, –

Julia   If you want me to leave, I will.

Tom   No. Erm. It's not that, it's just that –

Julia   I'm pregnant.

Tom   Pardon.

Julia   I'm having a baby. ... That was pretty much my reaction. Geoff and I didn't even like each other any more. Now he's gone. He doesn't know anything about it, yet. I will tell him but I don't want anything more to do with him and he doesn't want anything more to do with me. I couldn't promise he'd never visit but I can't see that lasting. So what do you think?

Tom   About what?

Julia   The baby.

Tom   Well, –, it's nothing to do with me.

Julia   Not directly, no. But events lead to events, and who says who causes those events, and time passes and time is used up, and you can't get that time back and we wanted one, you and I.

Tom   Yes.

Julia   We tried so hard and then –

Tom   Yes.

Julia   And after a bottle of wine, it seemed like the perfect solution. What d'you think?

Tom I er –

Jessica *walks out still with just her bra and skirt on.*

Julia Oh.

Jessica It's fine.

Julia Tom. You should have said.

Jessica I'll see you soon.

Tom No.

Jessica You have things to sort out.

Julia I'm so sorry.

Jessica May I have my top?

Julia What?

Jessica You're holding my top.

Julia Oh. Of course. Very pretty. I've one like this. My mother you see. I'm sorry. She died.

Jessica I heard. I'll see myself out.

Tom No. Please –

Julia If I'd known, honestly. ... Tom, I'm so sorry. ... I wouldn't have said, what I'd said –

Jessica *exits.*

Julia *follows her to try and explain.*

Tom *(to the audience)* I really wasn't expecting that. Right at that moment. Funny thing is Julia and I were going to go the whole hog, kids and everything. May not seem like I want them, wanted them, but I do, I did, desperately. I'd always imagined being a father, just not sure how I'd be if they weren't mine. We did the thing at the clinic, to check, when it wasn't working. Horrible stark room, big black vinyl chair with an industrial sized kitchen roll beside it. I had to check the door three times to make sure it was locked, that wasn't very conducive believe me, took me ages, a nurse even knocked on the door to ask if I was alright. That set me back further. I need the right atmosphere, as I said I'd have been, a better woman. Anyway I'm off the point, not sure how to deal with this. Jessica's gone home, Julia's upstairs. Seven years together, we were the established couple, hard to believe now, Morris and Sherry used to come to *us* for Sunday lunch. So Jessica, wild and a bit mad, what you see is what you get. I think. Julia, well, what *you* see is not what *I* got. I seem to remember. Jessica's got a child, someone else's. Julia's got a child, someone else's. What am I talking about, she slept with my boss. And look I've already forgotten about poor Amelia, perfect in every way but for the fact that she's dying, but we're all dying. A few good years might be best. There was always Veronica. She seemed nice. Sherry liked the sound of her and I liked Sherry once upon a time. Still do. ... I really wasn't expecting that ...

Scene Two

Tom's *house, the next morning (Sunday)*

Morris   ... Well, it would be an odd thing to be expecting. She still asleep?

Tom   I heard her snoring.

Morris   She snores?

Tom   A gentle snore though, nice snore. I popped my head round the door and Tilly's curled up at her feet. She ran out when she saw me. The cat not Julia. I don't let her on the bed. The cat not Julia.

Morris   How many women you slept with?

Tom   What?

Morris   You heard me.

Tom   You can't ask that.

Morris   Why not?

Tom   You just can't. At our age. How many have you slept with?

Morris   Two.

Tom   Two?

Morris   How many?

Tom   What difference does it make?

Morris   Doesn't. Just interested. Passing the time between coats.

Tom   Right. Two?

Morris   Two. So?

Tom   I don't know.

Morris   That many?

Tom   Not that many. I just don't keep count.

Morris   Work it out.

Tom   No.

Morris   Go on. Out of interest.

Tom   Why?

Morris   Go on.

Tom   Well, first one was obviously her.

Morris   Who, Sherry?

Tom   What? No. I've never slept with Sherry.

Morris   No, I know.

Act Two, Scene Two 69

Tom   Right. *(he tries to work it out)* Then there was er her, then her, her, her, her, no her then her, then there was er, her, her, her, um her, her, ... This is ridiculous.

Morris   Doesn't matter. Forget it. ... I love Sherry. ... Just wonder what gin and tonic might be like. Now and again. What d'you reckon to the colour now?

Tom   It's great.

Morris   Tis a bit brown.

Morris *eats a bit of Kendal Mint Cake.* **Sherry** *rushes in.*

Sherry   She wants you to be Geoff's baby's father?

Tom   Would have been a dream once. Apart from the Geoff bit. We had tried so hard to have one.

Sherry   But it didn't work? Obviously. Sorry. Silly.

Tom   Abnormal sperm. Never quite found out what that really meant. Distorted heads I think, with no sense of direction.

Morris   Sounds like the Conservative party. ... Not the best timing.

Tom   Three months ago this would have been a dream come true.

Morris   Yeah.

Sherry   Maybe.

Morris   She did do the dirty on you though, mate.

Tom   Who left who though? Maybe I emotionally withdrew so she was forced into his arms.

Sherry   Did she say that?

Tom*'s phone rings, he answers it.*

Tom   *(hoping it's* **Jessica***)* Hello. ... Oh. Sorry who? ... Nadine?

Sherry *looks at* **Morris**

Sherry   *(mouthing the word)* Nadine?

Morris   Guava.

Tom   Oh. I thought after our ... Oh. ... Did you? ... Oh ... Yes. It was. ... Sure. Bye. Bye.

Tom   *(puts the phone down)* Apparently she loved the kiss. I've got till tomorrow to ring her back or she's going out with Russell.

Sherry   Who's Russell?

Tom   I've no idea. What's going on? A week ago I had nobody. I'd been on my own for three years and no-one had shown the slightest interest. I was about to throw in the towel. Parents dead, no kids. Become one of those guys down the pub who pretend to work there and collect glasses. A quick, you know, once a week, if I can be bothered. Old age, in a home, slow eventual decline to death. Nothing achieved. No legacy. Not much point to my ever being here.

Morris   *(to* **Sherry***)* It's what I said.

Tom   And now it's like buses.

Morris   You've just got to choose which one to hop on.

Tom   Assuming I'm waiting at the right stop. I had made up my mind.

Sherry   Well, stick with it then.

Tom   But I loved Julia.

Sherry/Morris Yes.

Sherry   Since when though Tom? ... Since when did you love her?

Tom   Since always.

Sherry   Wouldn't you think, maybe, since she left you? Maybe?

Tom   No. I always loved her.

Morris   Yeah. Yeah, he did.

Sherry   OK.

Morris   Though we did have you round the odd evening when things weren't quite so great. Didn't we? Sometimes.

Tom   Oh yeah. I'm not saying it was perfect all the time. Whose relationship is? But I was in love. Wasn't I?

Sherry   I don't know, Tom.

Sherry *eats a bit of Kendal Mint Cake.*

Tom   I thought I was. Not sure.

Sherry   I'd forgotten how much I like this.

Tom   I saw a couple last week at the supermarket. They were working off the same shopping list but weren't paying full attention to each other. And at exactly the same moment they leant over and tried to grab the same box of cereal. They looked at each other and laughed. He gave her a quick kiss and went in search of eggs. That seemed like love. Do you think there's something they're getting that I wasn't?

Sherry   I don't know what you were getting.

Morris   Don't ask me.

Tom   Everyone I've met there's some complication.

Sherry   They'll always be something.

Tom   One woman's profile I read said she wanted a man with no baggage. I thought then, no baggage? How can you have no baggage at our age? Someone with no baggage would have to be a complete moron. That's what I've been looking for. No baggage. I've

	been looking for a complete moron. ... But actually what I imagined I wanted was someone sorted, dealt with their baggage. In the past.
Morris	Like you, you mean?
Tom	Interesting because of it not stifled by it. They had to be younger than me, had to be intelligent, attractive, sexy, funny, no kids. Christ a woman like that would be dating George Clooney. What was I expecting? I mean look at me.
Sherry	What do you mean?
Morris	He's got a point.
Tom	I'm alright I suppose, I have my own house, teeth mostly, a pretty average job and that's about it. Average man with average prospects seeks drop dead gorgeous A-list woman. And the older I've got the higher I've set my sights. By the time I hit eighty I'll be wanting Audrey Hepburn.
Morris	Dig her up and you can have her.
Tom	I don't know what the point is now.
Morris	The point is, being on your own is shit, being with someone is better.
Sherry	Beautifully put Morris.
Morris	And it's like us, it'd be like er getting rid of Saddam Hussein.
Tom	What would?
Morris	Divorce.
Tom	What?
Sherry	Divorce is like getting rid of Saddam Hussein?
Morris	No, not divorce. Not being together. Marriage.
Sherry/Tom	What?

Act Two, Scene Two 73

Morris   Well, the glue that the marriage is. Like keeping together all those factions, it was only after he'd gone did we find out what lurked beneath the surface. The rules, the not being able to get out of it.

Sherry   You can get out of it.

Morris   I don't want to get out of it. What I'm saying –

Sherry   Yes, what are you saying?

Morris   Is that if you're in a bad marriage say. Which we're not. And you think, I know I'll get out of it. Once upon a time that was pretty much a no no but these days it's easy. Relatively. So people bale at the least thing. And when they do they think the grass is going to be greener and like Tom has discovered it's not.

Tom   I've never been married.

Morris   Yeah but that's not the point, is it?

Tom   Isn't it?

Morris   Together then, not just marriage. But what I'm saying is that marriage covers up –

Sherry   Covers up?

Morris   Protects you against all the other bad things like loneliness, lack of self esteem.

Tom   I don't lack self esteem.

Tom *exits.*

Morris   No, Tom, I don't mean –. I mean you have to do everything yourself. Don't you? No job sharing. No sex. And always having to think about what's going to happen next, who you're going to meet. Marriage stops you thinking about –

Sherry   Marriage stops you thinking?

Morris   Stop twisting my words.

Sherry	I think you're doing that perfectly well all by yourself. Look if you want to go dating, you're a free man.
Morris	What? I'm saying the opposite.
Sherry	You're saying marriage is a prison.
Morris	No I'm not.
Sherry	Well, you're released. You've done nothing but lust over all his options. Christ, what happens if I fancy seeing someone else?
Morris	What are you saying?
Sherry	Maybe it's not all about you, have you thought about that?
Morris	You've got this all wrong.
Sherry	Maybe I'd like to see who's out there, maybe that's why we're not having enough sex, maybe I just don't want to. ... No, sorry.
Morris	No, you've said it now. You don't want to? What with me?
Sherry	I didn't mean that.
Morris	Well, you did last night.
Sherry	Yes.
Morris	What, going through the motions?
Sherry	Very rapidly.
Morris	What do you expect by day nine? You only have to practically look at me by then. And hang on it was your fault anyway. You know what happens when you do that. You know it. You were the one wanting it over and done with. Because you don't want to with me?
Sherry	I didn't mean it.

Morris Well, you've just fucking said it, that didn't come from nowhere. Well, I'll let you into a secret you've become, just between you and I, you've become –

Sherry It's 'between you and me'! It's always 'between you and me'.

Morris You said it. I never was educated enough for you.

Sherry You were educated plenty, just didn't bother to learn.

Morris You used to love my rough edges and bad boy image.

Sherry Bad boy? You lived in Godalming. ... I've become what?

Morris Sorry?

Sherry You were saying ... you've become ... I've become ... What?

Morris I er. I –

Sherry What have I become?

Morris I –, I –, I can't remember. You interrupted. Look, I'm sorry if wanting to make love to my wife is considered such an awful thing.

Sherry Rubbing up against me isn't my idea of making love.

Morris What's wrong with having sex? You used to love having sex. If I remember, wanted it more than me once upon a time. When did that stop?

Sherry When you make me feel guilty.

Morris About what?

Sherry Doing it all the time because you'd done that.

Morris We'd done that.

Sherry Well, –

Morris Being sliced open so we could have a sex life without the consequences of going through all that pain and

	hope and excitement and loss and loss, again and again. Consequences that you now just casually bring up. Sorry if that makes you feel guilty.
Sherry	Beholden.
Morris	I thought it would be flattering knowing I still want to have sex with you.
Sherry	That men want to fuck us is a done deal. We've known that since we were fourteen. Doesn't make us feel special.
Morris	I wouldn't mind feeling special.
Sherry	I'm constantly saying nice things to you.
Morris	When? I can't remember. You used to worship me.
Sherry	I still do.
Morris	Wouldn't hurt to show it now and again.
Sherry	Hero worship? Surely you're beyond that. I wouldn't mind some hearts and flowers.
Morris	Surely you're beyond that. I'm sorry but I want to have sex with you more!
Sherry	Any port in a storm.
Morris	What sort of sordid analogy is that? You see I can use the word analogy, I'm not thick just because I pronounce the haitch in haitch.
Sherry	It's an idiom not an analogy. And look at me Morris. Look at me closely. I'm a woman. Not a man. We're different.
Morris	I'm not stu –
Sherry	We're just different. I need wooing. It's in my DNA. You bought me a kettle, a cookery book and a rubbish bin for my birthday.
Morris	As well as a dress.

Act Two, Scene Two 77

Sherry　　I chose that.

Morris　　Otherwise it wouldn't have been the right one.

Sherry　　You have to take a risk.

Morris　　Well, we both know what happens when I do that, you take it straight back.

Sherry　　Not always.

Morris　　And why do we always have to go to Sicily on holiday.

Sherry　　What's that got to do with the price of fish? You love it there.

Morris　　We could go somewhere different.

Sherry　　As long as you don't grumble.

Morris　　I don't grumble.

Sherry　　You always grumble. If you grumbled less we could risk somewhere new.

Morris　　I don't grumble. ... I don't. ... What are we arguing about?

Sherry　　I don't know. I really don't know. *(repeating the question from earlier in the argument)* What have I become?

Pause

Morris　　Settled.

*This hits **Sherry** at her core.*

Julia *walks in wearing **Tom**'s pyjama bottoms and a T shirt, she looks like 'how could he have let this one go?'.*

Julia　　Sorry. Is it over? Have you finished?

Sherry　　Julia.

Julia　　Hi Sherry. Morrie. Very nice to see you. Been far too long.

Morris　　Yes. Long time.

Julia	Has he told you? ... Has he?
Morris	Um. Sherry?
Julia	Good. Thought I'd wake up this morning and think it was a crazy idea. Blame it on the wine. I've never behaved so rashly. I've been in the Lake District. Which is fine for a holiday but believe me you wouldn't want to live there. All anyone talks about is going up Scafell.
Sherry	We did Helvellyn.
Morris	And a walk around a lake.
Sherry	Derwent Water in autumn, beautiful colours.
Julia	Have that on repeat and you've pretty much summed up the conversation. So what do you think?
Sherry	About what?
Julia	Tom and me.
Sherry	Us?
Julia	Yes, you. We were a bit of foursome. Our cocktail and curry nights. The pub that time forgot. We could have that back.
Sherry	Yes.
Morris	Well, the pub hasn't changed.
Julia	But how would you feel?
Sherry	Well, we'd –, Morrie?
Morris	What?
Julia	It is a bit much to take in so quickly but time isn't on my side.
Sherry	No. Straight to the point Julia, don't always remember you being this direct.
Julia	He did tell you about the baby?

Act Two, Scene Two 79

Sherry Yes. Congratulations.

Morris Yes. Congratulations.

Julia So what do you think?

Sherry Well, as much as –, it's not really –. It's um. Isn't it Morrie?

Morris Yes. No. It's not –. It's Tom, isn't it?

Sherry Yes. Tom.

Julia But you'd both be fine?

Sherry Us? Well, we'd be delighted, wouldn't we?

Morris Yes.

Sherry But it doesn't matter about us.

Morris Who cares about us?

Julia Well, Tom does. I do obviously. You're bound to be involved.

Morris Are we? Yes. ... We do love babies.

Sherry Yes. We do. But it may not be that simple, now.

Morris Oh yes. Things aren't so simple now.

Julia Oh you mean the woman last night. How long's he been seeing her?

Sherry I er –. It's er –. Not sure how long.

Julia More than a month?

Sherry Er. Morrie?

Julia Didn't seem his type.

Sherry Well, we've hardly –

Julia And you know Tom, takes him forever to make up his mind about anything. When we went to the zoo he

	spent ages choosing between the penguins and the reptiles.
Sherry	Did he?
Julia	I said it doesn't matter which one you go to first you can go to the other one after.
Sherry	Right.
Julia	And he hates the zoo anyway, only went there because I wanted to, that's another thing, he does things for people when he doesn't really want to.
Sherry	Is that such a –?
Julia	You don't know where you stand, I mean you can be in the middle of a discussion about anything and he changes his point. Arguing one thing and then the other thing then back to his original thing depending on what he thinks *you* think about the thing. Why doesn't he just say what *he* thinks about the thing?
Sherry	Julia.
Julia	Why doesn't he just say it? Why doesn't he –?
Sherry	Julia. Are you alright?
Julia	Yes I'm fine. ... No I'm not.
Sherry	Sit down. Can I fetch you something?
Julia	I'm bloody stupid, aren't I? What am I doing? I'm pregnant. I'm behaving like a fucking pregnant hormonal lunatic. Christ I drank all that wine last night. I could have damaged the poor little mite. Oh shit. Never done anything like that before. I just started driving, I told myself I'd turn back but I just kept going. I don't even really like kids, *(apologising to the baby)* sorry, but I will. I will. Thing is I only tried with Tom because –, he did tell you we'd tried?
Sherry	Yes.

Act Two, Scene Three 81

Julia It was him really, I wanted one for him. Well, for us. Something that would be ours, it felt like we needed cement that would keep us together but unfortunately he had er, don't know if he told you, he had er –

Sherry/Morris Abnormal sperm.

Julia We didn't even find out what that really meant.

Morris Distorted heads I think ...

Sherry ... with no sense of direction.

Julia Seemed like the perfect solution. Is this woman serious?

Morris God, hardly. ... Oh I see what you mean.

Sherry We don't know.

Julia Christ. I know you probably hate me, –

Sherry No.

Julia – I'd hate me but I did love Tom. I promise you. It wasn't all my fault, you probably think it was but it wasn't. It wasn't. It wasn't. It wasn't –.

Julia *sobs,* **Sherry** *looks for something to wipe her eyes, the only thing* **Morris** *can find is a dirty painting cloth.*

Where is Tom?

Scene Three

Tom's *house / Various outside locations. Continuous.*

Tom *appears. From now on all scenes on stage are in play at the same time,* **Tom** *has the ability to be in both.*

Tom *(to the audience)* I'm waiting at the bus stop. The number 272 is due in – *(he looks at the display)* – three minutes.

Sherry Tom! Tom!

Tom It stops right outside Jessica's door.

Sherry *exits in search of* **Tom**. **Julia** *continues to cry.* **Morris** *is helpless.* **Julia** *grabs her bag and rummages through for hankies. She comes across a picture and hands it to* **Morris** *but in doing so drops on the floor an image of the scan of the baby.*

Julia What d'you think? ... Not that one. That's a baby. This.

Morris *(impressed)* That's –

Julia Yes, I was pleased.

Morris Photoshopped?

Julia No.

Morris Really?

Julia Pre-exposed background.

Morris Very Ansel Adams.

Julia Thank you.

Morris *(he means this)* It's stunning. Oh yes, beautiful.

Julia I bought a Nikon.

Morris You'll never go back.

Julia You liked me, didn't you?

Morris Of course I did.

Julia Did you think I was a bit odd?

Morris We're all a bit odd.

Julia I was at that time. Thing is. I know you're Tom's best friend –

Morris That's Sherry.

Julia – and I respect that but Tom doesn't do the spontaneous, the making a girl more important than anyone else. Geoff came along and he pursued me.

Act Two, Scene Three 83

> Relentlessly. If you think I gave in at first glance you'd be wrong. But I understand Tom more than anyone else. I was with him for seven years. I know why he says one thing but means another. I recognise every inflection with its hidden agenda. Tom could never escape my knowledge of him. And he shrunk away. I knocked on his door over and over and he shrunk away.

Tom *(looking at the bus stop display)* Still three minutes.

Julia There's probably this new one knocking on his door again imagining she'll change him. But she won't. So I've come back knowing that. I wasn't strong enough for both of us back then but now there's this I think I can be. Things can be different. There's something about Tom for me and there's something about me for him. My picture's still hanging there. That must mean something. He'll never give me all I need, I know, but that's alright. I think.

Morris You're not going to need him as much as you think. You're going to be a mum. That will take you over, utterly. I've watched it. It's the thing that scared me the most. Being superfluous. Often just getting in the way. So you won't be fighting over which way is best. It'll have its advantages.

Morris *exits in search of* **Sherry**.

Through the following, **Julia** *sits, sees the iPad with the profiles of* **Tom***'s dates and flicks through them.*

Tom *(to the audience)* That's progress knowing when a bus is going to turn up. A train, you look at the line and know you're connected, know that it will come, at some point, but a bus is different. I'm in the process of trying to get in touch with what my whole body really wants. I've been told many times that I think too much. So I'm attempting not to think. Which is easier said than done. When the bus turns up I'm going to see if I get on and go to Jessica's or I don't and go back inside and make coffee with Julia. *(he looks at the bus stop display)* Ah, two minutes ... Have you heard the one about the dog, the parrot and the Greek philosopher? Actually, no, that's not very funny. Have you heard the one about the –? That's a bit sexist. ... Never criticise someone until you've walked a mile in their shoes, that way when you criticise them you'll be a mile away and you'll have their shoes. That's one from my fridge. Talking of Greek philosophers. Plato put forward the theory that originally, way back, whenever that was, that each person was round, spherical, because they were actually made up of two people facing away from each other linked like acrobats in a tumbling routine. And that we were either all male, two men, descending from the sun; all female, two women, from the earth; or androgynous, one of each, from the moon. And we became so powerful we had the temerity to make an assault on the gods. Zeus was incensed but not wanting to lose our devotion, split us all in two and cast us to the four corners. And now we're left wandering the earth in terror of the gods searching for our other half to make ourselves whole and strong again. Trouble is we've never ever seen their face. But our body should know.

(he looks at the bus stop display) Four minutes. Four minutes!? Beginning to rain.

Sherry *returns with hankies and gives them to* **Julia**.

Julia *(referring to the profiles)* They all look like me.

Sherry We'd spotted that.

Julia Where is Tom?

Tom I'm here. Who'd like coffee?

Sherry *declines,* **Julia** *indicates that she would.*

Julia *takes the handkerchiefs and blows her nose.*

Tom *(to the audience)* I believe, right up to the point before you choose to take a look, an electron can be in two places at the same time. You really do have to feel for that electron.

Tom *(is now outside **Jessica**'s house calling up to an imagined open first floor window)* Jessica.

Julia *hands* **Sherry** *a small image scan of the baby.* **Sherry** *is reluctant to look at it.*

Julia Look. My baby. How did I get all the way to my age and get pregnant now? I used to be so careful. Oh, maybe that was it. *(**Sherry** is holding back tears and makes to leave)* Where are you going?

Sherry I'm fine.

Tom *(shouting up)* Jessica.

Julia Sherry?

Sherry *exits.*

Tom Jessica, please.

Jessica *appears. She is in her bathrobe.*

Tom I've been knocking.

Jessica I was in the shower.

Tom I thought you weren't talking to me.

Jessica Why? Just because your cheating ex has been knocked up by this sleaze bag and wants you to be her protector of the realm, after three years of absence.

Tom Are you fine about that?

Jessica About her asking? ... I'm over the moon. In her position I'd do the same. Actually no I wouldn't. I just said that.

Tom	What would you do?
Jessica	Anything but that.
Tom	May I come in?
Jessica	No.
Tom	Oh.
Jessica	Ella's in there.
Tom	Oh. It's raining.
Jessica	It's spitting. ... Wait there. *(she goes to leave, then decides to hand him a newspaper to protect him from the rain and gives him her coffee)* Don't go anywhere.

Jessica *exits.*

Julia	Tom, did you sleep well?

Tom *turns and is with* **Julia** *now.*

Tom	Not really.
Julia	Me neither.

Tom *hands* **Julia** *the coffee.*

Tom	Sugar?
Julia	Just milk. *(seeing the newspaper)* Still doing the crossword?
Tom	Not so much since we lost Araucaria.
Julia	That was very sad. He was the best. *(referring to the coffee)* You don't remember how I take it?
Tom	I do. Didn't want to put it in then –. Just making absolutely sure.
Julia	I know. ... Palace are doing better.
Tom	Are they?

Act Two, Scene Three 87

Julia You don't know? Oh. Do you not still go? Shame. No wonder you've lost weight, no more of those delicious dodgy burgers. ... So how are things? Generally.

Tom Fine.

Julia How's our little Tilly?

Tom On her last legs, I think.

Julia Oh no, really?

Tom Yeah. Fraid so. She's got a weepy eye and keeps sneezing.

Julia Oh dear. Poor Tilly. ... How's work?

Tom Pretty good. ... I got Geoff's job.

Julia Right.

Tom Silver lining.

Julia How's the pub that time forgot?

Tom Still the same. ... How's um –? How's –? ... How's your mum?

Julia Dead.

Tom Oh God sorry. Sorry.

They both begin to see the funny side to this.

Julia Tom –

Tom I'm so sorry.

Julia – you're priceless.

Tom I'm getting old. 'How's your mum?'

Julia As well as could be expected.

Tom Stop it.

Julia Under the circumstances.

Tom I'm so sorry.

Sherry *returns with the baby scan image.*

Sherry I'm really sorry, it's just that these ... *(seeing* **Tom***)* Oh.

Tom May I?

Tom *takes the picture and looks at it.*

Sherry Sorry.

Sherry *exits, still distressed.*

Julia Is she alright? ... It was seeing that which flipped me over the edge.

Tom Is it a boy or a girl?

Julia They couldn't tell, wrong angle. George for a boy, Ella for a girl.

Tom Ella?

Julia Don't you remember?

Tom Ella? Is that what we said?

Julia You don't remember.

Tom Is coffee alright?

Julia Coffee?

Tom You drinking. For the baby.

Julia Isn't it?

Tom I don't know.

Julia Better not then.

Tom A peppermint tea, perhaps? I think I might have some camomile –

Julia You're in this new relationship. I didn't know. I'm sorry. I'll get dressed and go.

Tom It's not a –

Julia What? Not a what?

Act Two, Scene Three

Tom Not a –. Well, it's –

Julia A casual thing?

Tom Just wouldn't call it a relationship quite yet. Not quite yet.

Julia *(repeating a phrase from their shared past)* Once you've slept with them Tom. Once you've slept with them.

Tom Yep.

Julia You have slept with her? I didn't bungle in on your first – ... Christ. God, I'm sorry. That must –. Sorry.

Tom You weren't to know.

Julia So you haven't –?

Tom I'm not comfortable with this conversation.

Julia No. No. Of course not. Timing. Though she's probably just one in a long line since me.

Tom Yes.

Julia I'm sure you've been making a barnful of hay in the past three years.

Jessica *appears.*

Jessica Tom! Tom! ... She's just getting it, hang on.

Jessica *exits.*

Julia Tom, last thing I want to do is upset anything you've got going on here. If it's going on, here. But if it's –. I mean I could stay with Dad for a while. If you're not –, you know. And we could, you know. Just see each other. A bit.

Tom *pops a bit of Kendal Mint Cake in his mouth.*

Tom Your dad? You'd kill each other.

Julia He's too lost to hate me, now Mum's gone.

Tom Oh is she –? Sorry. Overplay that joke.

Julia But I bet nobody's done that better than me.

Tom What?

Julia *(indicating his crotch area with a nod)* That.

Tom *now realising starts to choke on the Kendal Mint Cake.* **Julia** *is immediately on high alert.* **Tom** *puts his arm out to indicate to her not to say or do anything. He struggles for breath. There is a silent moment of pure tension which is broken by ..*

Tom It's OK. I'm OK.

Julia Oh God. Don't do that to me again.

Tom *recovering.*

Tom Just got caught.

Tom *lets out a sigh, he's alright. They look at each other remembering when this happened before.*

Tom/Julia *(remembering together)* Chew it.

Julia Thank God for the NHS.

Tom Though without you.

Julia So you owe me.

Tom Huh.

Tom *looks at her.*

Julia What?

Tom I realised I haven't looked at you properly.

They look at each other. Eventually ...

Julia I'm lost Tom. I shouldn't be here. I'm a complete mess. Tell me to fuck off. I beg you. For your own sake. Tell me to go.

Tom Your –

Julia   What?

Tom   Your erm –, your –

He indicates that her night wear has become a little loose at the top and she is inadvertently revealing herself to him, he averts his eyes and she covers herself up.

Julia   God. Sorry.

Tom   Perhaps you ought to get dressed.

Julia   Yes. Yes. Unfair to tempt you like that until you've bought the goods.

Tom   I had bought.

Julia   No you hadn't.

Jessica *arrives back with a package wrapped within an inch of its life using blue and red insulating tape.*

Jessica   Tom.

Tom *goes to hand the picture back.*

Julia   Keep it, I have another.

Julia *exits to get dressed.*

Tom *runs back to* **Jessica**, *his newspaper covering his head as if from the rain.*

Jessica   Here.

Jessica *hands* **Tom** *the package.*

Tom   What is it?

Jessica   It's from Ella.

Tom   What?

Jessica   Oh, there's a card.

Jessica *exits to get the card.*

Tom *(to the audience)* Thing is, this is now, you only know now. If I only knew now, this is who I imagine you'd be routing for. *(he indicates the wrapped package would be the choice)* But you don't know the seven years we were together.

Tom *thinks.*

Sherry *(offstage)* Morris!

Morris *enters.* **Sherry** *follows.*

Sherry Don't sulk.

Morris I wasn't.

Sherry How about India?

Morris India? That's a bit –

Sherry Yes, it is.

Morris The toilets. And the begging.

Sherry Yes.

Morris I *do* like Sicily.

Sherry So do I.

Morris Us is OK you know. Us plus one isn't the only answer.

Sherry I know.

Morris Because this is all I've got Sherry. Just this.

Sherry I know.

Morris So *do* you still worship me?

Sherry I do. ... Come on. It's up to us to set a good example. *(she holds her hand out for him to take)* We're what they're aspiring to.

Morris *takes her hand and they both exit.*

Tom *(to the audience)* Trouble is *I* don't know the seven years we were together. Not really. What did we do? How did we behave? What did I feel as I padded round the house getting ready for work? I can no more remember individual days than I can picture –, what her nipples were like. What were they like? Christ. They'd no longer be mine anyway. I could be a father. Like everyone else. Saturday morning, football or ballet. *(looking at the scan)* A brand new little baby.

Jessica *returns with the card.*

Tom What is it?

Jessica I have no idea. She made me swear on her granny's life that I wouldn't look. Then she wrapped it up so tight that I couldn't.

Tom How did she know I was coming?

Jessica She didn't. It's not for you. Not specifically. It's for whoever. Here's the card that goes with it.

Jessica *hands him the card and takes back his failed attempt at opening the package.*

Tom Why are you giving it to me?

Jessica There is a man who wont leave me alone. He's tall, fairly good looking, quite interesting, with a son a few years younger than Ella.

Tom Oh God, is that –?

Jessica What?

Tom *(indicating ... is he inside?)* Is he –?

Jessica I left you eight hours ago.

Tom Sorry.

Jessica He keeps ringing. He's sort of perfect for me and I'm tempted. ... And I'm really pissed off with you now.

Tom Sorry.

Jessica Eight hours.

Tom   Sorry.

Jessica   So God knows why –, *(referring to the eight hours)* fucking hell, ... why I'm hanging around for a slightly fucked up guy with OCD.

Tom   OCD?

Jessica   And I can't tell you why apart from the fact that I just felt something. I'm in touch with that feeling and I'm equally in touch with knowing that you're not. You have no certainty and that's bizarrely alluring. Up to a point. For God's sake give it here.

She takes the card from **Tom** *and rips it open then hands it back.*

Tom   *(reading)* 'Happy Birthday.' It's not my birthday.

Jessica   We've got hundreds of those. What's she written?

Tom   *(reading)* 'Dear dot dot dot, stroke, to whom it may concern. My mother is having a mid life crisis and is going out and getting drunk with lots of men'.

Jessica   Some.

Tom   *(reading)* 'Last night she came home and smashed her favourite pig ornament against the wall and then started wailing and banging on the door, and the other day she didn't come home till five o'clock in the morning'.

Jessica   Both times with you.

Tom   *(reading)* 'I know this because she tripped over the mat and woke me up. I couldn't get back to sleep which pissed me off –'

Jessica   She gets pissed off a lot.

Tom   *(reading)* ' – and I had double maths that day, which I hate. If you don't believe me ask her to show you her left knee. Now Mr. dot dot dot, if you haven't walked out by now and left her sitting at the bar drinking a huge vat of white wine then you can read on. And please note my mum doesn't sip wine she gulps it like water. She's a lush. Would you now open the box which should have unbroken red and blue tape all around it?'

Jessica *has ripped the box open and hands it to* **Tom**.

Julia *arrives back, dressed now.*

Julia   It was always our dream.

Tom   And I always wanted to be a father.

Julia   I know you did.

Jessica   I'm not asking for that.

Julia *exits in search of her coat.*

The box is now open she hands it to **Tom**. *Inside is a wilted carrot, parsnip and stick of celery.*

Tom   *(reading)* 'Never ever feed me any of these. Even if they are mashed up in a bowl of soup I will know. Yours faithfully, Ella.

Jessica   We're a package deal.

Tom   We've known each other a week.

Jessica   Time isn't on our side.

Tom   I can't have children.

Jessica   An entire relationship in three dates. You can't have children?

Tom   I've got abnormal sperm.

Jessica   What's wrong with it?

Tom   It's abnormal.

Jessica   You can't have children?

Tom	No. Think I might be a bit shit at sex too. Certainly to start with, though I definitely improve. So you might be better off picking the tall guy.
Jessica	Let me think about this.
Tom	Sure. I understand it's a big thing to –
Jessica	Ssh. *(she silences him and thinks for a few moments)* No, it's you I want.
Tom	What?
Jessica	It's you I want.
Tom	Did you decide that just then?
Jessica	Yes.
Tom	How?
Jessica	I just did.
Tom	But that's huge.
Jessica	Is it?
Tom	I'd have been walking around for weeks with something like that. How did you do it?
Jessica	I told you I either know or I don't. You really don't get this do you? You can't feel it. This. Can you? This thing. Here. It's clear as day to me. And you just don't get it. So now's your chance to break the habit of a lifetime. Me or Julia?
Tom	Well, –

Julia *enters, coat on, ready to leave.*

Julia	You can always change your mind.
Tom	But –

Julia *takes her lipstick out of her bag and applies it.*

Jessica   Difficult, isn't it? Three dates versus seven years. I could suggest you went away and thought about it. Which is what I know you want to do. But even after pacing the floor for weeks it will still boil down to a single moment's leap of faith. So that moment then is going to be the same as this moment now. The chasm won't narrow with time. Do you not trust what you feel?

Tom   *(he thinks)* No.

Jessica   Hah. I don't trust how I'll behave but I never doubt how I feel. Why not jump and just see how it goes? You can always change your mind.

Tom   No.

Julia   You can always change your mind.

Tom   No! I can't.

*(both women look at **Tom**)* I have to get it right.

(to the audience) This is the moment in the film just before he realises who he truly wants. The music swells, he turns and looks glassy eyed into the mid distance, a series of sepia toned memories are replayed of all the wonderful things she's ever done, and, crescendo, the penny drops. And he's off, a mad happily ever after dash across town to claim his prize before she gets on the plane with narcissistic Nigel and his pearly white teeth. Or does he arrive at the crossroad and have to choose? Which girl? Turn left for unknown stroppy actress, turn right for Jennifer Lawrence. Or does he walk coolly away with that killer line knowing she's putty in his hands? Hollywood has done more to ruin people's lives than two world wars. ... I have to get it right.

Julia   Sunday morning in bed.

Jessica   Look, if you don't want this, let's leave it.

Julia   Walks in the park.

Jessica   I'm not waiting forever.

Julia   We could get a dog.

Jessica   It's up to you.

Julia *and* **Jessica** *exit.*

Tom   *(to the audience)* I've heard it said, never go back. ... So I didn't. I sent Julia home, pregnant and in tears. I didn't have another date with Amelia, that felt harsh, I hope she's alright. I chose Jessica. Or truth be she chose me. Women always choose, whatever we think. It's all down to them. I've never had certainty so I'm relying on hers. We've been seeing each other a few months now. She is slightly mad, I think, not at all the type of woman I was expecting to end up with. Something about her though.

Jessica *comes on carrying Ella's school bag and coat.*

Jessica   Would you? I'm running late. *(She hands the bag and coat to* **Tom***, then kisses him)* To be continued, beautiful man.

Jessica *exits.*

Tom   *(to the audience)* I took Ella to school today. For the first time. I took her on my own. In my car. I had to ask her three times to put on her seat belt. In the end she did. Then we drove there and I tried to engage her in conversation but she wanted to listen to her music and text her friends, which she did. Then she took off her seat belt again to reach her bag from the back and I had to remind her to put it back on. She seemed reluctant as we were almost at her school. But she did. Then when I pulled up, she jumped out and ran across the road. Shouting 'thank you' as she went. I got out of the car and watched her as she went down the little lane and into the school gates. I waited until she'd passed the teacher on duty before getting back in the car. And I sat there. I couldn't move. And then I cried. I've never felt so responsible for someone in all my life.

(looks at the audience, takes a deep breath and lets out a thoughtful sigh)

Something about her though.

Fade to black.

www.ingramcontent.com/pod-product-compliance
Lightning Source LLC
LaVergne TN
LVHW041633070426
835507LV00008B/597